Differentiating Instruction With Menus

for the Inclusive Classroom

Math

Differentiating Instruction With Menus

for the Inclusive Classroom

Math

Laurie E. Westphal

PRUFROCK PRESS INC.
WACO, TEXAS

Library of Congress Cataloging-in-Publication Data

Westphal, Laurie E., 1967-
 Differentiating instruction with menus for the inclusive classroom. Math (grades 6-8) / by Laurie E. Westphal.
     pages cm
 Includes bibliographical references.
 ISBN 978-1-59363-964-8 (paperback)
 1. Mathematics--Study and teaching (Elementary) 2. Individualized instruction. 3. Inclusive education. 4. Mixed ability grouping in education. I. Title.
 QA135.6.W4743 2013
 510.71'2--dc23

                    2012019592

Edited by Sarah Morrison

Production design by Raquel Trevino

ISBN-13: 978-1-59363-964-8

At the time of this book's publication, all facts and figures cited are the most current available; all telephone numbers, addresses, and website URLs are accurate and active; all publications, organizations, websites, and other resources exist as described in this book; and all have been verified. The author and Prufrock Press make no warranty or guarantee concerning the information and materials given out by organizations or content found at websites, and we are not responsible for any changes that occur after this book's publication. If you find an error or believe that a resource listed here is not as described, please contact Prufrock Press.

Prufrock Press Inc.
P.O. Box 8813
Waco, TX 76714-8813
Phone: (800) 998-2208
Fax: (800) 240-0333
http://www.prufrock.com

CONTENTS

Author's Note

If you are familiar with books on various differentiation strategies, then you probably know about my Differentiating Instruction With Menus series, and you may be wondering about the differences between that series and this one, the Differentiating Instruction With Menus for the Inclusive Classroom series. In fact, when we first discussed creating this series, my editor asked how we could avoid having one series "cannibalize" (graphic, but a great word!) the other. Well, here is how I envision the two series being used:

These two series stand on their own if:
- You teach mostly lower ability, on-level, and ESL students and would like to modify your lessons on your own to accommodate a few advanced students. In this case, use this series, Differentiating Instruction With Menus for the Inclusive Classroom.
- You teach mostly advanced and high-ability students and would like to modify your lessons on your own to accommodate a few lower level students. In this case, use the Differentiating Instruction With Menus series.

These two series can serve as companions to one another if:
- You teach students with a wide range of abilities (from special education to gifted) and would benefit from having a total of three menus for a given topic of study: those for lower ability and on-level students (provided by this series, Differentiating Instruction With Menus for the Inclusive Classroom) and those for high-ability students (provided by the Differentiating Instruction With Menus series).

The menu designs used in this book reflect a successful modification technique I began using in my own classroom as the range of my students' ability levels widened. I experimented with many ways to use menus, from having students of all ability levels using the same menu with the same expectations, to having everyone using the same menu with modified contracted expectations, to using leveled menus where each student received one of three menus with some overlapping activities based on readiness, abilities, or preassessment results. I found that if the students in a given classroom had similar ability levels, I could use one menu with every student with slight modifications; however, the greater the span of ability levels, the more I needed the different leveled menus to reach everyone. Each book in the Differentiating Instruction With Menus for the Inclusive Classroom series has two leveled menus for the objectives covered: a lower level menu indicated by a ▲ and an on-level menu indicated by a ●. This way, teachers can provide more options to students with diverse abilities in the inclusive classroom. If used with the corresponding book in the Differentiating Instruction With Menus series, the teacher has a total of three leveled menus to work with.

Many teachers have told me how helpful the original Differentiating Instruction With Menus books are and how they have modified the books' menus to meet the needs of their lower level students. Teachers are always the first to make adjustments and find solutions, but wouldn't it be great if they had these preparations and changes already made for them? This is the purpose of the Differentiating Instruction With Menus for the Inclusive Classroom series.

—Laurie E. Westphal

CHAPTER 1

Choice in the Inclusive Middle School Classroom

> "When it comes to my sixth-grade math classroom, who *isn't* my audience?"
>
> *—Sixth-grade teacher, when asked to describe her target audience during a menu-writing session*

Let's begin by addressing the concept of the inclusive classroom. The term inclusive (vs. exclusive) leads one to believe that we are discussing a situation in which all students are included. In the simplest of terms, that is exactly what we are referring to as an inclusive classroom: a classroom that may have special needs students, on-level students, bilingual or ESL students, and gifted students. Although the concept is a simple one, the considerations are significant.

When thinking about the inclusive classroom and its unique ambiance, one must first consider the needs of the range of students within the classroom. Mercer, Lane, Jordan, Allsopp, and Eisele (1996) stated it best in their assessment of the needs in an inclusive classroom:

Students who are academically gifted, those who have had abundant experiences, and those who have demonstrated proficiency with lesson content typically tend to perform well when instruction is anchored at the "implicit" end of the instructional continuum. In contrast, low-performing students (i.e., students at risk for school failure, students with learning disabilities, and students with other special needs) and students with limited experience or proficiency with lesson content are most successful when instruction is explicit. Students with average academic performance tend to benefit most from the use of a variety of instructional methods that address individual needs. Instructional decisions for most students, therefore, should be based on assessment of individual needs. (pp. 230–231)

Acknowledging these varied and often contradictory needs that arise within an inclusive classroom can lead to frustration when trying to make one assignment or task fit everyone's needs. There are few—if any—traditional, teacher-directed lessons that can be implicit, explicit, and based on individual needs all at the same time. There is, however, one technique that tries to accomplish this: choice.

Choice: The Superman of Techniques in the Inclusive Middle School Classroom?

> ### "I like being able to choose. I can pick what I am good at!"
> —*Eighth-grade social studies student*

Can the offering of appropriate choices really be the hero of the inclusive middle school classroom? Can it leap buildings in a single bound and meet the needs of our implicit, explicit, and individual interests? Yes. By considering the use and benefits of choice, we can see that by offering choices, teachers really can meet the needs of the whole range of students in an inclusive classroom. Ask adults whether they would prefer to choose what to do or be told what to do, and of course, they will say they would prefer to have a choice. Students have the same feelings. Although they may not be experienced in making choices, they will make choices based on their needs, just as adults do—which makes everyone involved in the inclusive experience a little less stressed and frustrated.

Why Is Choice Essential to Middle School Students?

> "Almost every kid my age wants to be able to choose what they want to work on. They just do."
>
> —Eighth-grade math student, when asked if he thought choice was important in his classes

When considering the appropriateness of choice for middle school students, no matter their ability level, we begin by considering who (or what) our middle school students personify. During their years in middle school, adolescents struggle to determine who they are and how they fit into the world around them. They constantly try new ideas (that peroxide in the hair sounded like a good idea at the time!), new experiences (if you sit on the second-floor roof of your home one more time, I will tell your parents!), and a constant flux of personalities (preppy one day, dark nails and lipstick the next) in order to find themselves. During this process, which can take anywhere from a few months to a few years, depending on the child, children don't always have academics at the forefront of their minds. Thus, instruction and products have to engage the individuals whom these students are trying to become.

The Benefits of Choice

> "I am different in the way I do stuff. I like to build stuff with my hands."
>
> —Sixth-grade student, when asked why he enjoyed activities that allow choice

One benefit of choice is a greater sense of independence for the students, including some who have not had the opportunity to think about their own learning in the past. What a powerful feeling! Students will be designing and creating products based on what they envision, rather than what their teacher envisions. There is a possibility for more than one "right" product; all students can make products their own, no matter their level of ability. When students would enter my middle school classroom, they had often been trained by previous teachers to produce exactly what the teacher wanted, not what the students thought would be best. Teaching my students that what they envisioned could be correct (and wonderful) was often a struggle. "Is this what you want?" and "Is this right?" were popular questions as we started the school year. Allowing students to have choices in the products they create to demonstrate their learning helps create independence at any age, within any ability level.

> ## "[Choice] puts me in a good mood to participate!"
> —Seventh-grade student

Middle school students already have started transitioning from an academic focus to more of a social one. Choice is a way to help bring their focus back to the more desired (at least from everyone else's point of view) academic aspect of school. When students have choices in the activities they wish to complete, they are more focused on the learning that leads to their chosen products. Students become excited when they learn information that can help them develop a product they would like to create. Students pay close attention to instruction and have an immediate application for the knowledge being presented in class. Also, if students are focused, they are less likely to be off task during instruction.

The final benefit (although I am sure there are many more) is the simple fact that by offering varied choices at appropriate levels, you can address implicit instructional options, explicit instructional options, and individual needs without anyone getting overly frustrated or overworked. Many a great educator has referred to the idea that the best learning takes place when the students have a desire to learn and can feel successful while doing it. Some middle school students still have a desire to learn anything that is new to them, but many others do not want to learn anything unless it is of interest to them. By choosing from different activities according to their interests and readiness, students stretch beyond what they already know, and by offering such choices, teachers create a void that needs to be filled. This void leads to a desire to learn.

A Point to Ponder: Making Good Choices Is a Skill

> ## "It's a good point. How can we expect children to make good choices when they haven't had the chance to make any yet?"
> *– Eighth-grade teacher, after hearing me discuss choice as a skill*

When we think of making a good choice as a skill, much like writing an effective paragraph, it becomes easy enough to understand the processes needed to encourage students to make their own choices. In keeping with this analogy, students could certainly figure out how to write on their own, and perhaps even how to compose sentences and paragraphs, by modeling other examples. Imagine, however, the progress and strength of the writing produced when students are given guidance and even the most basic of instructions on how to accomplish the task. The written piece is still their own, but the quality of the finished piece is much stronger when guidance is given during the process. The same is true with the quality of choices students can make in the classroom.

As with writing, students—especially those with special needs—could make choices on their own, but when the teacher provides background knowledge and assistance, the choices become more meaningful and the products richer. Although all students certainly need guidance, on-level and special needs students often will need the most guidance; they have usually not been in an educational setting that has allowed them to experience different products, and the idea of choice can be new to them. Some students may have experienced only basic instructional choices, like choosing between two journal prompts or perhaps having the option of making either a poster or a PowerPoint presentation about the content being studied. Some may not have experienced even this level of choice. This lack of experience may cause frustration for both teacher and student.

Teaching Choices as a Skill

So, what is the best way to provide guidance and enable middle school students to develop the skill of making good choices? First, identify the appropriate number of choices for your students. Although the goal might be to have students choose from 20 different options, teachers might start by having their students select from a smaller number of predetermined choices the first day (if they were using a Game Show menu, for instance, students might choose one activity from the first column). Then, after that product had been created, students could choose from another set of options a few days later, and perhaps from another set the following week. By breaking students' choices down, teachers reinforce how to approach or attack a more complex and/or varied choice format in the future. All students can work up to making complex choices from longer lists of options as their choice skill level increases.

Second, although our middle school students feel they know everything, they may still need guidance on how to select the option that is right for them (and not select something just because their friends select it!). They may not automatically gravitate toward options without an exciting and detailed description of each choice. For the most part, students have been trained to produce what the teacher requests, which means that when given a choice, they will usually choose what seems to be the easiest and what the teacher most wants (then they can get to what they would prefer to be doing). This means that when the teacher discusses the different menu options, he or she has to be equally as excited about each option. The discussion of the different choices has to be animated and specific. For example, if the content is all very similar, the focus should be on the product: "If you want to do some singing, then this one is for you!" or "If you want to write and draw, then check this one as a maybe!" Sometimes, options may differ based on both content and product, in which case both can be pointed out to students to assist them in making good choices for themselves. "You have some different choices in our ecosystems unit. If you want to do something with animals and the computer, then check this one as a maybe. If you are thinking you want to do something with specimen collecting and making an exhibit, then this one might be for you." The more exposure students have to the processing the teacher provides, the more skilled they become at making good choices.

How Can Teachers Provide Choices?

> "I was concerned at first that my students would be confused by so many options and that their focus and behavior might be impacted. Instead, they really responded well—I am going to encourage other teachers to use menus for choice."
>
> *—Middle school inclusion teacher, when asked how her students with special needs responded to having choices*

When people go to a restaurant, the common goal is to find something on the menu to satisfy their hunger. Students come into our classrooms having a hunger, as well—a hunger for learning. Choice menus are a way of allowing our students to choose how they would like to satisfy that hunger. At the very least, a menu is a list of choices that students use to choose an activity (or activities) they would like to complete to show what they have learned. At best, it is a complex system in which students earn points by making choices from different areas of study. All menus should also incorporate a free-choice option for those "picky eaters" who would like to make a special order to satisfy their learning hunger.

The next few sections provide examples of the main types of menus that will be used in this book. Each menu has its own benefits, limitations or drawbacks, and time considerations. An explanation of the free-choice option and its management will follow the information on each type of menu.

Meal Menu

> "My students appreciate and need choices. At first, they may need fewer at a time."
>
> *—Middle school inclusion teacher, when asked about her students with special needs having choices*

Description

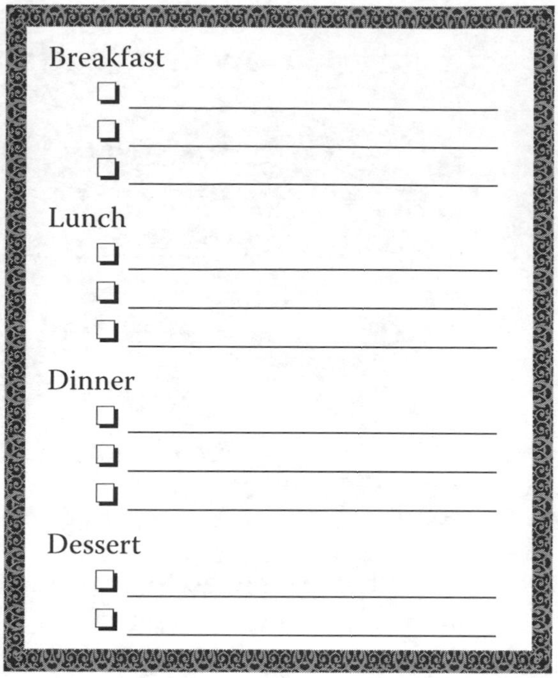

The Meal menu (see Figure 1.1) is a menu with a total of at least nine predetermined choices as well as two or more enrichment options for students. The choices are created at the various levels of Bloom's Revised taxonomy (Anderson & Krathwohl, 2001) and incorporate different learning styles, with the levels getting progressively higher as students move from breakfast to lunch and then on to dinner. All products carry the same weight for grading and have similar expectations for completion time and effort. The enrichment (dessert) options can be used for extra credit or can replace another meal option at the teacher's discretion.

Breakfast

❏ _____
❏ _____
❏ _____

Lunch

❏ _____
❏ _____
❏ _____

Dinner

❏ _____
❏ _____
❏ _____

Dessert

❏ _____
❏ _____

Figure 1.1. Meal menu.

Benefits

User friendliness. This menu is very straightforward and easy to understand for students with special needs.

Flexibility. This menu can cover either one topic in depth or three different objectives, with each meal representing a different objective. With this menu, students have the option of completing three products: one from each meal.

Optional enrichment. Although the dessert category is not required, this part of the Meal menu allows students to have the option of going further or deeper if time permits.

Easily broken down. The Meal menu is very easy to break apart into smaller pieces for students who need support in making choices. Students could be asked to select a breakfast option while the rest of the menu is put on hold; then, once the breakfast product is submitted, they could select a lunch option, and so on.

Friendly design. Students quickly understand how to use this menu because of its real-world application.

Weighting. All products are equally weighted, so recording grades and maintaining paperwork are easily accomplished with this menu.

Short time period. This menu is intended for shorter periods of time, between 1–3 weeks.

Limitations

Few topics. This menu only covers one or three topics.

Time Considerations

This menu is usually intended for shorter periods of completion time—at most, it should take 3 weeks. If the menu focuses on one topic in depth, then it can be completed in one week.

Tic-Tac-Toe Menu

> "[Tic-Tac-Toe menus] can be a real pain. A lot of times I only liked two of the choices and had to do the last one. Usually I got stuck with a play or a presentation."
>
> —Sixth-grade math student, when asked to step out of her comfort zone based on the tic-tac-toe design

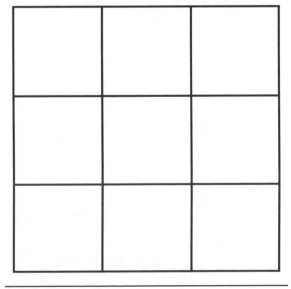

Description

The Tic-Tac-Toe menu (see Figure 1.2) is a well-known, commonly used menu that contains a total of eight predetermined choices and, if appropriate, one free choice for students. Choices can be created at the same level of Bloom's Revised taxonomy or can be arranged in such a way to allow for three different levels or content areas. If all choices have been created at the same level of

Figure 1.2. Tic-Tac-Toe menu.

Bloom's Revised taxonomy, then each choice has similar expectations for completion time and effort.

Benefits

Flexibility. This menu can cover either one topic in depth or three different topics, objectives, or even content areas. When this menu covers just one objective and all tasks are from the same level of Bloom's Revised taxonomy, students have the option of completing three projects in a tic-tac-toe pattern, or simply picking three from the menu. When the menu covers three objectives or different levels of Bloom's Revised taxonomy, students will need to complete a tic-tac-toe pattern (either a vertical column or horizontal row) to be sure they have completed one activity from each objective or level.

Stretching. When students make choices on this menu, completing a row or column based on its design, they will usually face one choice that is out of their comfort zone, be it for its Bloom's Revised taxonomy level, its product learning style, or its content. They will complete this "uncomfortable" choice because they want to do the other two in that row or column.

Friendly design. Students quickly understand how to use this menu. It is nonthreatening because it does not contain points, and therefore it seems to encourage students to stretch out of their comfort zones.

Weighting. All projects are equally weighted, so recording grades and maintaining paperwork is easily accomplished with this menu.

Short time period. This menu is intended for shorter periods of time, between 1–3 weeks.

Limitations

Few topics. This menu only covers one or three topics.

Student compromise. Although this menu does allow choice, a student will sometimes have to compromise and complete an activity he or she would not have chosen because it completes the required tic-tac-toe. (This is not always bad, though!)

Time Considerations

This menu is usually intended for shorter amounts of completion time—at the most, it should take 3 weeks with one product submitted each week. If the menu focuses on one topic in depth, it can be completed in one week.

List Menu

"I like that you can add up the points to be more than 100, so even if you make some small mistakes, your grade could still be a 100."

—Seventh-grade student

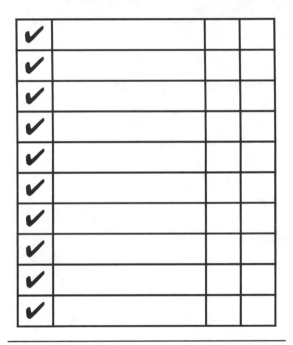

Figure 1.3. List menu.

Description

The List menu (see Figure 1.3), or Challenge List, is a more complex menu than the Tic-Tac-Toe menu, with a total of at least 10 predetermined choices, each with its own point value, and at least one free choice for students. Choices are simply listed with assigned points based on the levels of Bloom's Revised taxonomy. The choices carry different weights and have different expectations for completion time and effort. A point criterion is set forth that equals 100%, and students choose how they wish to attain that point goal.

Benefits

Responsibility. Students have complete control over their grades. They really like the idea that they can guarantee their grades if they complete the required work. If they lose points on one of the chosen assignments, then they can complete another to be sure they have met their goal points. This responsibility over their own grades also allows a shift in thinking about grades: whereas many students think of grades in terms of how the teacher judged their work, having control over their grades leads students to understand that they earn them.

Different learning levels. This menu also has the flexibility to allow for individualized contracts for different learning levels within the classroom. Each student can choose what products will provide the points for his or her 100%.

Concept reinforcement. This menu allows for an in-depth study of material; however, with the different levels of Bloom's Revised taxonomy being represented, students who are still learning the concepts can choose some of the lower level point value projects to reinforce the basics before jumping into the higher level activities.

Variety. A List menu offers a larger variety of product choices. There is guaranteed to be a product of interest to everyone.

Limitations

One topic. This menu is best used for one topic in depth, so that students don't miss any specific content.

Cannot guarantee objectives. If this menu is used for more than one topic, it is possible for a student to not complete an activity for each objective, depending on the choices he or she makes.

Preparation. Teachers need to have all materials ready at the beginning of the unit for students to be able to choose any of the activities on the list, which requires advanced planning. (Note: Once the materials are assembled, the menu is wonderfully low stress!)

Time Considerations

This menu is usually intended for shorter amounts of completion time—at the most, 2 weeks.

20-50-80 Menu

> "My least favorite menu is 20-50-80. You can't just do the easy ones. If you pick a 20, then you have to do an 80. No matter what, you have to do one of the hard ones."
>
> *—Seventh-grade student*

Figure 1.4. 20-50-80 menu.

Description

A 20-50-80 menu (see Figure 1.4) is a variation on a List menu, with a total of at least eight predetermined choices: two choices with a point value of 20, at least four choices with a point value of 50, and at least two choices with a point value of 80. Choices are assigned points based on the levels of Bloom's Revised taxonomy. Choices with a point value of 20 represent the "remember" and "understand" levels, choices with a point value of 50 represent the "apply" and "analyze" levels, and choices with a point value of 80 represent the "evaluate" and "create" levels. All levels of choices carry different weights and have different expectations for completion time and effort. Students are expected to earn 100 points for a 100%. Students choose what combination they would like to use to attain that point goal.

Benefits

Responsibility. With this menu, students still have complete control over their grades.

Guaranteed activity. This menu's design is also set up in such a way that students must complete at least one activity at a higher level of Bloom's Revised taxonomy in order to reach their point goal.

Great introductory menu. This menu is one of the shortest menus; if students choose well, they can accomplish their goal by completing only two products. This menu is usually less daunting than some of the longer, more complex menus. It provides students a great introduction to the process of making choices.

Limitations

One topic. Although it can be used for more than one topic, this menu works best with an in-depth study of one topic.

Higher level thinking. Students may choose to complete only one activity at a higher level of thinking.

Time Considerations

This menu is usually intended for a shorter amount of completion time—at the most, one week.

Baseball Menu

> ## "There were so many choices, and most of them were fun activities!"
>
> *—Sixth-grade student*

Description

The Baseball menu (see Figure 1.5) is a baseball-based variation of the List menu with a total of at least 20 predetermined choices: choices are given values as singles, doubles, triples, or home runs based on the levels of Bloom's Revised taxonomy. Singles represent the remember and understand levels; doubles, the apply and analyze levels; triples, the evaluate level; and home runs, the create level. All levels of choices carry different weights and have different expectations for completion time and effort. Students are expected to earn a certain number of runs (around all four bases) for a 100%. Students choose what combination they would like to use to attain that number of runs.

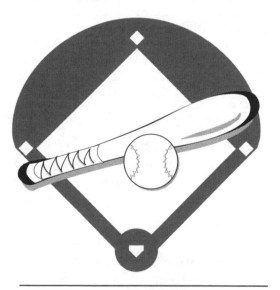

Figure 1.5. Baseball menu.

Benefits

Responsibility. With this menu, students still have complete control over their own grades.

Flexibility and variety. This menu allows for many choices at each level. Students should have no trouble finding something that catches their interest.

Theme. This menu has a fun theme that students enjoy and can be used throughout the classroom. A bulletin board can be set up with a baseball diamond, with each student having his or her own player who can move through the bases. Not only can students keep track of their own RBIs, but they can also have a visual reminder of what they have completed.

Limitations

One topic. This menu is best used for one all-encompassing unit with many objectives for in-depth study.

Preparation. With so many choices available to students, teachers should have all materials ready at the beginning of the unit for students to be able to choose any of the activities on the list. This sometimes causes a consideration for space in the classroom.

Time Considerations

This menu is usually intended for a longer amount of completion time, depending on the number of runs required for a 100%—at the most, 4 or 5 weeks.

Game Show Menu

> "This menu was very easy to break down for my [students needing modifications], as we could focus on just one column at a time. They were very successful with the format."
>
> —Seventh-grade science teacher

Description

The Game Show menu (see Figure 1.6) is a complex menu. It covers multiple topics or objectives with at least three predetermined choices and a free-choice option for each objective. Choices are assigned points based on the levels of Bloom's Revised taxonomy. All choices carry different weights and have different expectations for completion time and effort. A point criterion is set forth that equals 100%. Students must complete at least one activity from each objective in order to reach their goal.

Figure 1.6. Game Show menu.

Benefits

Free choice. This menu allows many choices for students, but if they do not want to complete the offered activities, they can propose their own activity for each objective.

Responsibility. This menu allows students to guarantee their own grades.

Different learning levels. This menu has the flexibility to allow for individualized contracts for different learning levels within the classroom. Each student can contract for a certain number of points for his or her 100%.

Objectives guaranteed. The teacher is guaranteed that the students complete an activity from each objective covered, even if it is at a lower level.

Limitations

Confirm expectations. The only real limitation for this menu is that students (and parents) must understand the guidelines for completing the menu.

Time Considerations

This menu is usually intended for a longer amount of completion time. Although it can be used as a yearlong menu (each column could be for one grading period), it is usually intended for 2–3 weeks.

Free Choice in the Inclusive Classroom

> "I didn't do one [free choice] on the menu. I didn't really get it, but I saw a poster [as a free choice] that my friend did that was really cool. I think I want to do a free choice on the next one."
>
> *—Seventh-grade inclusion student*

Most of the menus included in this book allow students to submit a free-choice product. This is a product of their choosing that addresses the content being studied and shows what the student has learned about the topic. Although this option is available, students may not fully understand its benefits or immediately respond to the opportunity even after it has been explained. In the past, certain students may have been offered choices and enjoyed the idea of taking charge of their own learning; however, students with special needs may not have had much exposure to this concept. Their educational experiences tend to be objective-based and teacher-driven. This is not to say that they would not respond well to the idea of free choice; in fact, they can embrace it as enthusiastically as gifted students can. The most significant difference between these two groups successfully approaching free choice is the amount of content needed by the student before he or she embarks on a proposed option. Students with special needs need to feel confident in their knowledge of the content and information before they are ready to step out on their own, propose their own ideas, and create their own products. Gifted students may be comfortable with less knowledge and structure.

With most of the menus, the students are allowed to submit a free-choice product for their teacher's consideration. Figure 1.7 shows two sample proposal forms that have been used successfully in my classroom. With middle school students, this cuts down greatly on the whining that often accompanies any task given to students. A copy of these forms should be given to each student when the menu is first introduced. The form used is based on the type of menu being presented. For example, if you are using the Tic-Tac-Toe menu, there is no need to submit a point proposal. A discussion should be held with the students so they understand the expectations of a free choice. I always had a few students who

Name: _____ Teacher's Approval: _____

Free-Choice Proposal Form for Point-Based Menu

Points Requested: _____ Points Approved: _____

Proposal Outline

1. What specific topic or idea will you learn about?

2. What criteria should be used to grade it? (Neatness, content, creativity, artistic value, etc.)

3. What will your product look like?

4. What materials will you need from the teacher to create this product?

Name: _____ Teacher's Approval: _____

Free-Choice Proposal Form

Proposal Outline

1. What specific topic or idea will you learn about?

2. What criteria should be used to grade it? (Neatness, content, creativity, artistic value, etc.)

3. What will your product look like?

4. What materials will you need from the teacher to create this product?

Figure 1.7. Sample proposal forms for free choice.

did not want to complete a task on the menu; students are welcome to create their own free-choice proposals and submit them for approval. The biggest complainers will not always go to the trouble to complete the form and have it approved, but it is their choice not to do so. The more free choice is used and encouraged, the more students will begin to request it. How the students show their knowledge will begin to shift from teacher-focused to student-designed activities. If students do not want to make a proposal using the proposal form after the teacher has discussed the entire menu and its activities, then they can place the unused form in a designated place in the classroom. Others may want to use their forms, and it is often surprising who wants to submit a proposal form after hearing about the opportunity!

Proposal forms must be submitted before students begin working on their free-choice products. The teacher then knows what the students are working on, and the student knows the expectations the teacher has for that product. Once the project has been approved, the form can easily be stapled to the student's menu sheet. The student can refer to the form while developing the free-choice product, and when the grading takes place, the teacher can refer to the agreement for the graded features of the product.

Each part of the proposal form is important and needs to be discussed with students:

- *Name/Teacher's Approval.* The student must submit this form to the teacher for approval. The teacher will carefully review all of the information, discuss any suggestions or alterations with the student, if needed, and then sign the top.
- *Points Requested.* Found only on the point-based menu proposal form, this is where negotiation may need to take place. Students usually will submit their first request for a very high number (even the 100% goal). They tend to equate the amount of time something will take with the number of points it should earn. But please note that the points are always based on the levels of Bloom's Revised taxonomy. For example, a PowerPoint presentation with a vocabulary word quiz would get minimal points, although it may have taken a long time to create. If the students have not been exposed to the levels of Bloom's Revised taxonomy, this can be difficult to explain. You can always refer to the popular "Bloom's Verbs" to help explain the difference between time-consuming and higher level activities.

- *Points Approved.* Found only on the point-based menu proposal form, this is the final decision recorded by the teacher once the point haggling is finished.
- *Proposal Outline.* This is where the student will tell you everything about the product he or she intends to complete. These questions should be completed in such a way that you can really picture what the student is planning to complete. This also shows you that the student knows what he or she plans to complete.
  - *What specific topic or idea will you learn about?* Students need to be specific here. It is not acceptable to write "science" or "reading." This is where students look at the objectives of the lesson and choose which objective their product demonstrates.
  - *What criteria should be used to grade it?* Although there are rubrics for all of the products that the students might create, it is important for the students to explain what criteria are most important to evaluate the product. The student may indicate that the rubric being used for all of the predetermined products is fine; however, he or she may also want to add other criteria here.
  - *What will your product look like?* It is important that this response be as detailed as possible. If a student cannot express what it will look like, then he or she has probably not given the free-choice plan enough thought.
  - *What materials will you need from the teacher to create this product?* This is an important consideration. Sometimes students do not have the means to purchase items for their project. This can be negotiated as well, but if you ask what students may need, they will often develop even grander ideas for their free choice.

CHAPTER 2

How to Use Menus in the Inclusive Classroom

There are different ways to use instructional menus in the inclusive classroom. In order to decide how to implement each menu, the following questions should be considered: How much prior knowledge of the topic being taught do the students have before the unit or lesson begins, how confident are your students in making choices and working independently, and how much intellectually appropriate information is readily available for students to obtain on their own? After considering these questions, there are a variety of ways to use menus in the classroom.

Building Background Knowledge

> "I have students with so many different experiences—sometimes I spend a lot more time than I allotted to review and get everyone up to speed before we get started."
>
> —*Seventh-grade social studies teacher*

There are many ways to use menus in the classroom. One way that is often overlooked is using menus to review or build background knowledge before a unit begins. This is frequently used when students have had exposure to upcoming content in the past, perhaps during the previous year's instruction or through similar life experiences. In reality, most middle school students have had exposure to the basic information needed in their classes; however, students may not remember the details of the content well enough to proceed with the upcoming unit immediately. A shorter menu covering the background or previous year's objectives can be provided in the weeks prior to the new unit so that students have the opportunity to recall and engage with the information in a meaningful way. They will then be ready to take their knowledge to a deeper level during the unit. For example, 2 weeks before starting a unit on statistics, the teacher may select a short menu on mean, median, mode, and range, knowing that the students have covered the content in the past and should be able to successfully work independently on the menu by engaging their prior knowledge. Students work on products from the menu as anchor activities and homework throughout the 2 weeks preceding the statistics unit, with all products being submitted prior to the unit's initiation. This way, the students have been in the "statistics frame of mind" independently for 2 weeks and are ready to investigate the topic further.

Enrichment and Supplemental Activities

> "I wanted to start allowing some choice in my novel projects, so I chose a menu that matched each genre. It really worked well—the students worked on their projects every day when they had time."
>
> *–Sixth-grade language arts teacher*

Using the menus for enrichment and supplementary activities is the most common way of using menus. In this case, the students usually do not have a lot of background knowledge, and information about the topic may not be readily available to all students. The teacher will introduce the menu and the activities at the beginning of a unit. The teacher then will progress through the content at the normal rate using his or her curricular materials, periodically allowing class and homework time throughout the unit for students to work on their menu choices to supplement a deeper understanding of the lessons being taught. This method is very effective, as it incorporates an immediate use for the content the teacher is covering. For example, at the beginning of a unit on fractions, the teacher may introduce the menu with the explanation that students may not yet have all of the knowledge needed to complete their choices. During the unit, however, more content will be provided, and the students will be prepared to work on new choices. If students want to work ahead, they can certainly find the information on their own, but that is not required. Although some students often see this as a challenge and will begin to investigate concepts mentioned in the menu before the teacher has discussed them, other students begin to develop questions about the concepts and are ready to ask them when the teacher covers the material. This helps build an immense pool of background knowledge and possible content questions before the topic is even discussed in the classroom. As teachers, we constantly fight the battle of trying to get students to read ahead or come to class already prepared for discussion. By introducing a menu at the beginning of a unit and allowing students to complete products as instruction progresses, we encourage the students to naturally investigate the information and come to class prepared without having to make preparation a separate requirement.

Mainstream Instructional Activities

> "On your suggestion, I tried using the Game Show menu with my geometry unit because I had 3 days of instruction that the students knew well and could work on independently. They really responded to the independence."
>
> *—Eighth-grade math teacher*

Another option for using menus in the classroom is to replace certain curricular activities the teacher uses to teach the specified content. In this case, the students may have some limited background knowledge about the content and have information readily available for them among their classroom resources. This situation allows the teacher to pick and choose which aspects of the content need to be directly taught to the students in large or small groups and which can be appropriately learned and reinforced through product menus. The unit is then designed using formal instructional large-group lessons, smaller informal group lessons, and specific menu days during which the students use the menu to reinforce their prior knowledge. In order for this option to be effective, the teacher must feel very comfortable with the students' prior knowledge level and their readiness to work independently. Another variation on this method is using the menus to drive station activities. Stations have many different functions in the middle school classroom. They can contain activities that are best completed individually to reinforce the content being taught, or—a more common occurrence in middle school—they can allow students access to products or activities that may include specialized resources. Many classrooms may not have enough supplies or resources to set up eight versions of the same activity; however, by making different "resource-heavy" activities available at stations, students can experience the content while the teacher may only need one set-up of each activity.

Mini-Lessons

> "I have so many different levels in my classroom, using menus with mini-lessons has been a life saver. I can actually work with small groups, and everyone else doesn't run wild!"
>
> —*Eighth-grade math teacher*

Yet another option for menus is to use them with mini-lessons, with the menus driving the accompanying classroom activities. This method is best used when the majority of the students have similar amounts of knowledge about the topic. The teacher can design 15–20-minute mini-lessons in which students quickly review basic concepts that are already familiar to them and are then exposed to the new content in a short and concise way. Then students are turned loose to choose an activity on the menu to show that they understand the concept. The Game Show menu usually works very well with this method of instruction, as the topics across the top usually lend themselves to these mini-lessons. It is important that the students either have some prior knowledge of the content or are effective at working independently, because the lesson cycle is shorter in this use of menus. Using menus in this way does shorten the amount of time teachers have to use the guided practice step of the lesson, so all instruction and examples should be carefully selected. By using the menus in this way, the teacher avoids the one-size-fits-all independent practice portion of the lesson. If there are still a few students struggling, they can be pulled into a small-group situation while the other students work on their choices from the menu. Another important consideration is the independence level of the students. In order for this use of menus to be effective, students will need to be able to work independently for up to 30 minutes after the mini-lesson. Because students are often interested in the product they have chosen, this is not a critical issue, but it is still one worth mentioning as teachers consider how they would like to use various menus in their classrooms.

Introducing and Using Leveled Menus With Students

"That's not fair . . ."
—A middle school student somewhere in the world, this very minute

The menus in this book are tiered versions of the menus found in its companion series, Differentiating Instruction With Menus. Although the topics and objectives are alike, these menus may have different values assigned to the same tasks, slightly different wording for similar tasks, the same product options in a menu of a different format, or even tasks that are only available on certain menus. All of these minor modifications make certain menus more appropriate for different students based on their readiness, interests, and ability levels.

As we all know, middle school students tend to compare answers, work, and ideas, and the same goes for their menu choices. Although students may notice the slight aforementioned differences, it may not be an issue when students are working in ability groups, as students are comfortable with not having the exact same options as their classmates. It may also not be an issue when the menus are presented in a matter-of-fact manner, as everyone is getting a menu that was especially chosen for him or her, so students may notice some differences between their menus. Students should rest assured that target numbers (e.g., a goal of 100 points must be met to receive a 100%) is equal for all of the menus provided, and that the activities most often preferred by students are found on all of the menus. Students should also know that most of the menus have a free-choice proposal option, so if they really want to do one of the activities found on another menu in the classroom, they are welcome to submit a free-choice proposal form in order to complete that activity. By presenting tiered menus with confidence and by making it clear that each menu is selected specifically for each student, you can make students much more willing to accept the system and proceed within the confines that you have set.

That being said, you may still have a few students who say, in that dreaded nasal, accusatory, middle schooler's tone: "That's still not fair!" When I first starting using leveled menus with my eighth graders, I heard a few comments like this. They quickly dissipated with my standard and practiced responses. Of course, the first response (which they do not always appreciate) is that fair is not the same as equal. I know students do not like to hear this response, as it is patently true and therefore difficult to dispute. Secondly, I remind students that everyone has different strengths, and the menus are distributed in order to emphasize students' strengths. Again, they know this; they just do not like to acknowledge it. Lastly, if the students are being especially surly, I sometimes have to play the "parent card," meaning that I am the teacher and therefore have the right to do what I feel is best for each student. This last option is non-negotiable, and although students may not like it, they understand the tone and sentiment, as they have usually experienced it at home.

The bottom line when it comes to tiered menus is that students will respond to the use of different menus within a classroom based on how the teacher presents or reacts to the menus. In the past, when I have used different formats, I have addressed the format or obvious differences in a matter-of-fact manner, by saying things such as, "I have spiced things up with this menu and have three different ones that I will pass out. You may receive one that is different than your neighbor's, but whichever one you receive is going to be lots of fun for you!" Other times, when the menus are very similar in their formats and graphics, I simply distribute them and address concerns when they are brought up. For the most part, students are more likely to simply go with what they have been given when the differences in menus are presented confidently, without being open to debate or complaint.

CHAPTER 3

Guidelines for Products

> "I got to do a play! In math!"
>
> —*Seventh-grade student*

This chapter outlines the different types of products included in the featured menus, as well as the guidelines and expectations for each. It is very important that students know exactly what the expectations of a completed product are when they choose to work on it. By discussing these expectations before students begin and having the information readily available ahead of time, you will limit the frustration on everyone's part.

$1 Contract

> "The $1 contract sure cuts out those late-night trips to buy supplies for [my son's] products!"
>
> —*Sixth-grade teacher and parent of a middle schooler*

$1 Contract

I did not spend more than $1.00 on my _____.

_____   _____
Student Signature   Date

My child, _____, did not spend more than $1.00 on the product he or she created.

_____   _____
Parent Signature   Date

Figure 3.1. $1 contract.

Consideration should be given to the cost of creating the products featured on any menu. The resources available to students vary within a classroom, and students should not be graded on the amount of materials they can purchase to make a product look better. These menus are designed to equalize the resources students have available. The materials for most products are available for less than a dollar and can often be found in a teacher's classroom as part of the classroom supplies. If a product requires materials from the student, there is a $1 contract as part of the product criteria. This is a very important piece in the explanation of the product. First of all, by limiting the amount of money a child can spend, teachers create an equal amount of resources for all students. Second, this practice actually encourages a more creative product. When students are limited by the amount of materials they can readily purchase, they often have to use materials from home in new and unique ways. Figure 3.1 is a sample of the contract that has been used many times in my classroom with various products.

The Products

Table 3.1 contains a list of the products used in this book, along with ideas for other products that students may choose to develop as free-choice activities. These products were chosen for their flexibility in meet-

Table 3.1

Products

Visual	Kinesthetic	Auditory
Acrostic	Board Game	Children's Book
Advertisement	Bulletin Board Display	Commercial/Infomercial
Book Cover	Class Game	Game Show
Brochure/Pamphlet	Commercial/Infomercial	Interview
Bulletin Board Display	Concentration Cards	News Report
Cartoon/Comic Strip	Cross-Cut Diagram/Model	Oral Presentation of Created
Children's Book	Diorama	Product
Class Lesson—Written Only	Experiment	Play/Skit
Collage	Flipbook	PowerPoint—Speaker
Collection	Folded Quiz Book	Puppet
Cross-Cut Diagram/Model	Mobile	Song/Rap
Crossword Puzzle	Model	Speech
Data Table	Mural	Student-Taught Lesson
Drawing	Museum Exhibit	Video
Essay	Play/Skit	You Be the Person
Folded Quiz Book	Product Cube	Presentation
Graph	Puppet	
Graphic Novel	Quiz Board	
Greeting Card	Sculpture	
Instruction Card	Student-Taught Lesson	
Journal/Diary	Three-Dimensional Timeline	
Letter	Trophy	
Map	Video	
Mind Map		
Newspaper Article		
Paragraph		
Pie Graph		
Poster		
PowerPoint—Stand Alone		
Questionnaire		
Quiz		
Recipe Card		
Scrapbook		
Story		
Summary		
Survey		
Three Facts and a Fib		
Trading Cards		
Venn Diagram		
Video		
WebQuest		
Windowpane		
Worksheet		

ing different learning styles, as well as for being products many teachers are already using in their classrooms. They have been arranged by learning style—visual, kinesthetic, or auditory—and each menu has been designed to include products from all of these learning styles. Of course, some of the products may represent more than one style of learning, depending on how they are presented or implemented. Some of these products are featured in the menus more often than others, but students may choose the less common products as free-choice options.

Product Frustrations

One of the biggest frustrations that accompany the use of these various products on menus is the barrage of questions about the products themselves. Students can become so wrapped up in the products and the criteria for creating them that they do not focus on the content being presented. This is especially true when menus are introduced to the class. Students can spend an exorbitant amount of time asking the teacher about the products mentioned on the menu. When this happens, what should have been a 10–15-minute menu introduction turns into 45–50 minutes of discussion about product expectations. In order to facilitate the introduction of the menu products, teachers may consider showing students examples of the product(s) from the previous year. Although this can be helpful, it can also lead to additional frustration on the part of both the teacher and the students. Some students may not feel that they can produce a product as nice, as big, as special, or as (you fill in the blank) as the example, or when shown an example, students might interpret that as meaning that the teacher would like something exactly like the one he or she showed to students. To avoid this situation, I would propose that when using examples, the example students are shown be a "blank" one that demonstrates how to create only the shell of the product. If an example of a windowpane is needed, for instance, students might be shown a blank piece of paper that is divided into six panes. The students can then take the skeleton of the product and make it their own as they create their own version of the windowpane using their information.

Product Guidelines

Most frustrations associated with products can be addressed proactively through the use of standardized, predetermined product guidelines, to be shared with students prior to the creation of any products.

These product guidelines are designed in a specific yet generic way, such that any time throughout the school year that the students select a product, that product's guidelines will apply. A beneficial side effect of using set guidelines for a product is the security it creates. Students are often reticent to try something new, as doing so requires taking a risk. Traditionally, when students select a product, they ask questions about creating it, hope they remember and understood all of the details, and turn it in. It can be quite a surprise when they receive the product back and realize that it was not complete or was not what was expected. As you can imagine, students may not want to take the risk on something new the next time; they often prefer to do what they know and be successful. Through the use of product guidelines, students can begin to feel secure in their choices before they start working on new products. If they are not feeling secure, they tend to stay within their comfort zone.

The product guidelines for menu products included in this book, as well as some potential free-choice options, are presented in an easy-to-read card format (see Figure 3.2). (The guidelines for some products, such as summaries, are omitted because teachers often have their own criteria for these products.) Once the products and/or menus have been selected, there are many options available to share this information.

There really is no one right way to share the product guideline information with your students. It all depends on their abilities and needs. Some teachers choose to duplicate and distribute all of the product guidelines pages to students at the beginning of the year so that each child has his or her own copy while working on products. As another option, a few classroom sets can be created by gluing each product guideline card onto a separate index card, hole punching the corner of each card, and placing all of the cards on a metal ring. These ring sets can be placed in a central location or at stations where students can borrow and return them as they work on their products. This allows for the addition of products as they are introduced. Some teachers prefer to introduce product guidelines as students experience products on their menus. In this case, product guidelines from the menu currently assigned can be enlarged, laminated, and posted on a bulletin board for easy access during classroom work. Some teachers may choose to reproduce each menu's specific product guidelines on the back of the menu. No matter which method teachers choose to share the information with the students, they will save themselves a lot of time and frustration by having the product guidelines available for student reference (e.g., "Look at your product guidelines—I think that will answer your question").

Acrostic	Advertisement	Board Game
• Must be at least 8.5" by 11" • Neatly written or typed • Target word written down the left side of the paper • Each descriptive phrase chosen must begin with one of the letters from the target word • Each descriptive phrase chosen must be related to the target word	• Must be at least 8.5" by 11" • A slogan should be included • Color picture of item or service should be included • Include price, if appropriate • Can be created on the computer	• At least four thematic game pieces • At least 20 colored/thematic squares • At least 15 question/activity cards • Include a thematic title on the board • Include a complete set of rules for playing the game • At least the size of an open file folder
Book Cover	**Brochure/Pamphlet**	**Bulletin Board Display**
• Front cover—title, author, image • Front inside flap—paragraph summary of the book • Back inside flap—brief biography of author with at least three details • Back cover—your comments about the book • Spine—title and author	• Must be at least 8.5" by 11" • Must be in three-fold format; front fold has the title and picture • Must have both pictures and written text • Information should be in paragraph form with at least five facts included • Can be created on the computer	• Must fit within assigned space on bulletin board or wall • Must include at least five details • Must have a title • Must have at least five different elements (e.g., posters, papers, questions) • Must have at least one interactive element that engages the reader
Cartoon/Comic Strip	**Children's Book**	**Class Game**
• Must be at least 8.5" by 11" • Must have at least six cells • Must have meaningful dialogue • Must include color	• Must have a cover with book's title and student's name as author • Must have at least 10 pages • Each page should have an illustration to accompany the story • Neatly written or typed • Can be created on the computer	• Game should allow all class members to participate • Must have only a few, easy-to-understand rules • Can be a new variation on a current game • Must have multiple questions • Must provide answer key before game is played • Must be approved by teacher before being played

Figure 3.2. Product guidelines.

Class Lesson—Written Only	Collage	Collection
(Note: For a class lesson that is presented, use the student-taught lesson rubric.) • Is original—do not just print or copy an activity as is • States the objectives that will be taught • Includes at least one warm-up question • Presents the information in a clear way • Includes all of the important information • Has a way for students to practice the content • Includes a quiz or method of assessment	• Must be at least 8.5" by 11" • Pictures must be cut neatly from magazines or newspapers (no clip art from the computer or the Internet) • Label items as required in task	• Contains number of items stated in task • All items must fit in the space designated by the teacher • All items must be brought to class in a box or bag • No living things!
Commercial/Infomercial	**Concentration Cards**	**Cross-Cut Diagram/Model**
• Must be 1–2 minutes in length • Script must be turned in before the commercial is presented • Can be presented live to an audience or recorded • Should have props or some form of costume(s) • Can include more than one person	• At least 20 index cards (10 matching sets) • Both pictures and words can be used • Information should be placed on just one side of each card • Include an answer key that shows the matches • All cards must be submitted in a carrying bag	• Must include a scale to show the relationship between the diagram/model and the actual item • Must include details for each layer • If creating a diagram, must also meet the guidelines for a poster • If creating a model, must also meet the guidelines for a model
Crossword Puzzle	**Data Table**	**Diorama**
• At least 20 significant words or phrases should be included • Develop appropriate clues • Include puzzle and answer key • Can be created on the computer	• Table and data have proper units, titles, and descriptions • All data should be recorded neatly and be easy to read • If created by hand, all lines should be straight and neat	• Must be at least 4" by 5" by 8" • Must be self-standing • All interior space must be covered with relevant pictures and information • Name written on the back • Informational/title card attached to diorama • $1 contract signed

Figure 3.2. Continued.

Drawing	Essay	Experiment
• Must be at least 8.5" by 11" • Must show what is requested in the task statement • Must include color • Must be neatly drawn by hand • Must have title • Name written on the back	• Must be neatly written or typed • Must cover the specific topic in detail • Must be at least three paragraphs • Must include resources or bibliography if appropriate	• Includes a hypothesis or purpose • States specific materials for experiment • Includes detailed procedures and data • Includes a written conclusion in paragraph form • Information neatly written or typed as a report
Flipbook	**Folded Quiz Book**	**Game Show**
• Must be at least 8.5" by 11" folded in half • All information or opinions are supported by facts • Created with the correct number of flaps cut into the top • Color is optional • Name written on the back	• Must be at least 8.5" by 11" folded in half • Must have at least 10 questions • Created with the correct number of flaps cut into the top • Questions written or typed neatly on upper flaps • Answers written or typed neatly inside each flap • Color is optional • Name written on the back	• Needs an emcee or host • Must have at least two contestants • Must have at least one regular round and a bonus round • Questions will be content specific • Props can be used, but are not mandatory
Graph	**Graphic Novel**	**Greeting Card**
• Must have a title • Axes must be labeled with units • All data must be clearly represented • Can be created on the computer • If created by hand, must use graph paper	• Should use color • Must tell a story • Should be at least 10 pages in length • Can be created on the computer	• Front—colored pictures, words optional • Front inside—personal note related to topic • Back inside—greeting or saying; must meet product criteria • Back outside—logo, publisher, and price for card

Figure 3.2. Continued.

Instruction Card	Interview	Journal/Diary
• Must be no larger than 5" by 8" • Created on heavy paper or index card • Neatly written or typed • Uses color drawings • Provides instructions stated in the task	• Must have at least eight questions about the topic being studied • Person chosen for interview must be an "expert" and qualified to provide answers • Questions and answers must be neatly written or typed	• Neatly written or typed • Should include the appropriate number of entries • Should include a date if appropriate • Should be written in first person
Letter	**Map**	**Mind Map**
• Neatly written or typed • Uses proper letter format • At least three paragraphs in length • Must follow type of letter stated in the menu (e.g., friendly, persuasive, informational)	• Must be at least 8.5" by 11" • Accurate information is included • Includes at least 10 relevant locations • Includes compass rose, legend, scale, and key	• Must be at least 8.5" by 11" • Uses unlined paper • Must have one central idea • Follows the "no more than four" rule—no more than four words coming from any one word • Should be neatly written or developed using a computer
Mobile	**Model**	**Mural**
• Includes at least 10 pieces of related information • Includes color and pictures • At least three layers of hanging information • Hangs in a balanced way	• Must be at least 8" by 8" by 12" • Parts of model must be labeled • Should be in scale if possible • Must include a title card • Name should be permanently written on the model	• Must be at least 22" x 54" • Must contain at least five pieces of important information • Must have colored pictures • Words are optional, but a title should be included • Name should be permanently written on the back

Figure 3.2. Continued.

Museum Exhibit	News Report	Newspaper Article
• Should have title for exhibit • Must include at least five "artifacts" • Each artifact must be labeled with a neatly written card • Exhibit must fit within the size assigned • $1 contract required • No expensive or irreplaceable objects in the display	• Must address the who, what, where, when, why, and how of the topic • Script of report must be turned in with project (or before if performance will be live) • Must be either performed live or recorded	• Must be informational in nature • Must follow standard newspaper format • Must include picture with caption that supports article • At least three paragraphs in length • Neatly written or typed
Paragraph	**Pie Graph**	**Play/Skit**
• Neatly written or typed • Must have topic sentence, at least three supporting sentences or details, and a concluding sentence • Must use appropriate vocabulary and follow grammar rules	• Must have a title • Must have a label for each area or be color coded with a key • Must include the percentages for each area of the graph • Calculations must be provided if needed to create the pie graph • Should be created neatly by hand or using a computer	• Must be 4–6 minutes in length • Script must be turned in before play is presented • May be presented to an audience or recorded for future showing • Should have props or some form of costume(s) • Can include more than one person
Poster	**PowerPoint—Speaker**	**PowerPoint—Stand Alone**
• Should be the size of a standard poster board • Includes at least five pieces of important information • Must have title • Must contain both words and pictures • Name written on the back • Bibliography included as needed	• At least 10 informational slides and one title slide with student's name • No more than two words per page • Slides must have color and no more than one graphic per page • Animations are optional but should not distract from information being presented • Presentation should be timed and flow with the speech being given	• At least 10 informational slides and one title slide with student's name • No more than 10 words per page • Slides must have color and no more than one graphic per page • Animations are optional but should not distract from information being presented

Figure 3.2. Continued.

Product Cube	Puppet	Questionnaire
• All six sides of the cube must be filled with information • Neatly written or typed • Name must be printed neatly on the bottom of one of the sides • Should be submitted flat for grading	• Puppet should be handmade and must have a moveable mouth • A list of supplies used to make the puppet must be turned in with the puppet • $1 contract signed • If used in a puppet show, must also meet the criteria of a play	• Neatly written or typed • Includes at least 10 questions with possible answers, and at least one answer that requires a written response • Questions must be helpful to gathering information on the topic being studied
Quiz	**Quiz Board**	**Recipe Card**
• Must be at least a half sheet of paper long • Neatly written or typed • Must cover the specific topic in detail • Must include at least five questions including a short answer question • Must have at least one graphic • An answer key must be turned in with the quiz	• Must have at least five questions • Must have at least five answers • Should use a system with lights • Should be no larger than a poster board • Holiday lights can be used • $1 contract signed	• Must be written neatly or typed on a piece of paper or an index card • Must have a list of ingredients with measurement for each • Must have numbered steps that explain how to make the recipe
Scrapbook	**Sculpture**	**Song/Rap**
• Cover of scrapbook must have a meaningful title and student's name • Must have at least five themed pages • Each page will have at least one meaningful picture • All photos must have captions	• Must be no larger than 24" tall • Must use recycled materials • Must be created from the number of items given in the task • If appropriate, $1 contract must be submitted with sculpture • Creator's name should be permanently written on the base or bottom	• Words must make sense • Can be presented to an audience or taped • Written words must be turned in before performance or with taped song • Should be at least 2 minutes in length

Figure 3.2. Continued.

Speech	Story	Survey
• Must be at least 2 minutes in length • Should not be read from written paper • Note cards can be used • Written speech must be turned in before speech is presented • Voice must be clear, loud, and easy to understand	• Must have all of the elements of a well-written story (setting, characters, conflict, rising action, and resolution) • Must be appropriate length to allow for story elements • Neatly written or typed	• Must have at least five questions related to the topic • Must include at least one adult respondent who is not your teacher • The respondent must sign the survey • Information gathered and conclusions drawn from the survey should be written or presented graphically

Three-Dimensional Timeline	Three Facts and a Fib	Trading Cards
• Must be no bigger than standard-size poster board • Must be divided into equal time units • Must contain at least 10 important dates and have at least 2 sentences explaining why each date is important • Must have a meaningful object securely attached beside each date to represent that date • Must be able to explain how each object represents each date	• Can be written, typed, or created using PowerPoint • Must include exactly four statements: three true statements and one false statement • False statement should not obvious • Brief paragraph should be included that explains why the fib is false	• Include at least 10 cards • Each card must be at least 3" by 5" • Each should have a colored picture • Include at least three facts on the subject of the card • Cards must have information on both sides • All cards must be submitted in a carrying bag

Trophy	Venn Diagram	Video
• Must be at least 6" tall • Must have a base with the name of the person getting the trophy and the name of the award written neatly or typed on it • Top of trophy must be appropriate and represent the award • Name should be written on the bottom of the award • Must be an originally designed trophy (avoid reusing a trophy from home)	• Must be at least 8.5" by 11" • Shapes should be thematic and neatly drawn • Must have a title for entire diagram and a title for each section • Must have at least six items in each section of the diagram • Name written on the back	• Use VHS, DVD, or Flash format • Turn in a written plan with project • Students will need to arrange their own way to record the video or allow teacher at least 3 days notice to set up recording • Covers important information about the project • Name written on the video label

Figure 3.2. Continued.

WebQuest	Windowpane	Worksheet
• Must quest through at least three high-quality websites • Websites should be linked in the document • Can be submitted in a Word or PowerPoint document • Includes at least three questions for each website • Must address the topic	• Must be at least 8.5" by 11" unlined paper • Must include at least six squares • Each square must include both a picture and words that should be neatly written or typed • All pictures should be both creative and meaningful • Name should be written on the bottom right-hand corner of the front of the windowpane	• Must be 8.5" by 11" • Neatly written or typed • Must cover the specific topic or question in detail • Must have at least one graphic • An answer key will be turned in with the worksheet
You Be the Person Presentation • Take on the role of the person • Cover at least five important facts about the life of the person • Must be 3–5 minutes in length • Script must be turned in before information is presented • Should be presented to an audience with the ability to answer questions while in character • Must have props or some form of costume		

Figure 3.2. Continued.

CHAPTER 4

Rubrics

> "[Using menus,] I frequently end up with more papers and products to grade than with a unit taught in the traditional way. Luckily, rubrics speed up the process."
>
> *—Eighth-grade teacher*

The most common reason teachers feel uncomfortable with menus is the need for equal grading. Teachers often feel that it is easier to grade the same type of product made by all of the students than to grade a large number of different products, none of which looks like any other. The great equalizer for hundreds of different products is a generic rubric that can cover all of the important qualities of an excellent product.

All-Purpose Rubric

Figure 4.1 is an example of a rubric that has been classroom tested with the menus included in this book. This rubric can be used with any point value activity presented in a menu, as there are five criteria and the columns represent full points, half points, and no points.

There are different ways that this rubric can be shared with students. Some teachers prefer to provide it when a menu is presented to students. The rubric can be reproduced on the back of the menu along with its guidelines. The rubric can also be given to students to keep in their folders with their product guideline cards so they always know the expectations as they complete projects throughout the school year. Some teachers prefer to keep a master copy for themselves and post an enlarged copy of the rubric on a bulletin board, or provide one copy for parents during open house so that they understand how their children's menu products will be graded.

No matter how the rubric is shared with students, the first time they see this rubric, it should be explained to them in detail, especially the last column, titled "Self." It is very important that students self-evaluate their projects. This column can provide a unique perspective on the project as it is being graded. Note: This rubric was designed to be specific enough that students will understand the criteria the teacher is seeking, but general enough that they can still be as creative as they like while making their products.

Student-Taught Lesson Rubric

Although the all-purpose product rubric can be used for all activities, there is one occasion that warrants a special rubric: student-taught lessons. This situation has many fine details that must be considered separately.

Student-taught lessons can cause stress for both students and teachers. Teachers would often like to allow students to teach their fellow classmates, but they are not comfortable with the grading aspect of the assignment. Rarely do students understand all of the components that go into designing an effective lesson. This student-taught lesson rubric (see Figure 4.2) helps focus the student on the important aspects of a well-designed lesson and allows teachers to make the evaluation more subjective.

All-Purpose Rubric

Name: _____

Criteria	Excellent (Full Credit)	Good (Half Credit)	Poor (No Credit)	Self
Content Is the content of the product well chosen?	Content chosen represents the best choice for the product. Information or graphics are well chosen and related to content.	Information or graphics are related to content, but are not the best choice for the product.	Information or graphics presented do not appear to be related to the topic or task.	
Completeness Is everything included in the product?	All information needed is included. Product meets the product criteria and the criteria of the task as stated.	Some important information is missing. Product meets the product criteria and the criteria of the task as stated.	Most important information is missing. The product does not meet the task or does not meet the product criteria.	
Creativity Is the product original?	Presentation of information is from a new perspective. Graphics are original. Product includes elements of fun and interest.	Presentation of information is from a new perspective. Graphics are not original. Product has elements of fun and interest.	There is no evidence of new thoughts or perspectives in the product.	
Correctness Is all of the information included correct?	All information presented in the product is correct and accurate.		Any portion of the information presented in the product is incorrect.	
Communication Is the information in the product well communicated?	All information is neat and easy to read. Product is in appropriate format and shows significant effort. Oral presentations are easy to understand and presented with fluency.	Most of the product is neat and easy to read. Product is in appropriate format and shows significant effort. Oral presentations are easy to understand, with some fluency.	The product is not neat and easy to read or the product is not in the appropriate format. It does not show significant effort. Oral presentation was not fluent or easy to understand.	
			Total Grade:	

Figure 4.1. All-purpose product rubric.

Student-Taught Lesson Rubric

Name: _____

Parts of Lesson	Excellent	Good	Fair	Poor	Self
Prepared and Ready All materials and lesson ready at start of class period, from warm-up to conclusion of lesson.	**10** Everything is ready to present.	**6** Lesson is present, but small amount of scrambling.	**3** Lesson is present, but major scrambling.	**0** No lesson ready or missing major components.	
Understanding Presenter understands the material well. Students understand information presented.	**20** All information is correct and in correct format.	**12** Presenter understands; 25% of students do not.	**4** Presenter understands; 50% of students do not.	**0** Presenter is confused.	
Complete Includes all significant information from section or topic.	**15** Includes all important information.	**10** Includes most important information.	**2** Includes less than 50% of the important information.	**0** Information is not related.	
Practice Includes some way for students to practice or access the information.	**20** Practice present; well chosen.	**10** Practice present; can be applied effectively.	**5** Practice present; not related or best choice.	**0** No practice or students are confused.	
Interest/Fun Most of the class is involved, interested, and participating.	**15** Everyone interested and participating.	**10** 75% actively participating.	**5** Less than 50% actively participating.	**0** Everyone off task.	
Creativity Information presented in an imaginative way.	**20** Wow, creative! I never would have thought of that!	**12** Good ideas!	**5** Some good pieces but general instruction.	**0** No creativity; all lecture, notes, or worksheet.	
				Total Grade:	

Your Topic/Objective:

Comments:

Don't Forget:
All copy requests and material requests must be made at least 24 hours in advance.

Figure 4.2. Student-taught lesson rubric.

The Menus

How to Use the Menu Pages

Each menu in this section has:
- an introduction page for the teacher;
- a lower level content menu, indicated by a triangle (▲) in the upper right-hand corner;
- an on-level content menu, indicated by a circle (●) in the upper right-hand corner;
- any specific guidelines for the menu; and
- activities mentioned in the menu.

Introduction Pages

The introduction pages are meant to provide an overview of each menu. They are divided into five areas:

1. *Objectives Covered Through These Menus and These Activities.* This area will list all of the objectives that the menus can address. Menus are arranged in such a way that if students complete the guidelines set forth in the instructions for the menus, all of these objectives will be covered.

2. *Materials Needed by Students for Completion.* For each menu, it is expected that the teacher will provide, or students will have access to, the following materials:
   - lined paper;
   - glue;
   - crayons, colored pencils, or markers; and
   - blank 8.5" x 11" white paper.

   The introduction page also includes a list of additional materials that may be needed by students as they complete either menu. Any materials listed that are used in only one of the two menus are designated with the menu's corresponding code (either triangle or circle). Students do have the choice about the menu items they can complete, so it is possible that the teacher will not need all of these materials for every student.

3. *Special Notes on the Use of These Menus.* This section will give any special tips on managing student products as well as any specific modification suggestions. This section will also share any tips to consider for a specific activity.

4. *Time Frame.* Most menus are best used in at least a 1-week time frame. Some are better suited to more than 2 weeks. This section will give an overview about the best time frame for completing the entire menu, as well as options for shorter time periods. If teachers do not have time to devote to an entire menu, they can certainly choose the 1–2-day option for any menu topic students are currently studying.

5. *Suggested Forms.* This is a list of the rubrics, templates, and reproducibles that should be available for students as the menus are introduced. If a menu has a free-choice option, the appropriate proposal form also will be listed here.

CHAPTER 5

Numbers and Operations

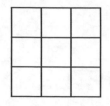

Problem Solving

Meal Menu ▲ and Tic-Tac-Toe Menu ●

Objectives Covered Through These Menus and These Activities

- Students will identify different ways to solve problems.
- Students will evaluate different problem-solving techniques and their effectiveness.
- Students will create a method of remembering problem-solving strategies for the future.
- Students will evaluate the reasonableness of answers.

Materials Needed by Students for Completion

- Poster board or large white paper
- Blank index cards (for trading cards and concentration cards)
- Materials for bulletin board display ●
- Paper bags (for puppets) ▲
- Socks (for puppets) ▲
- Microsoft PowerPoint or other slideshow software ▲
- Materials for class games ●

Special Notes on the Use of These Menus

This topic has two different menu formats: Meal menu and Tic-Tac-Toe menu. The Meal menu is specifically selected for its meal-oriented, Bloom's-based options, as it is easily broken into manageable bits. The menu can be cut into strips, each strip featuring its own meal, to be given to students. This way, once students have chosen and submitted the breakfast product for grading, they can move on to the lunch strip, and lastly, they can complete the dinner and dessert strips. Because this type of menu is designed to become more advanced as students move through the meals, teachers may choose to provide their students who have special needs with just the meals and save the dessert for enrichment.

These menus allow students to create a bulletin board display. Some classrooms may only have one bulletin board, so the teacher can divide the board into sections, or additional classroom wall or hall space can be sectioned off for the creation of these displays. Students can plan their displays based on the amount of space they are assigned.

The circle menu gives students the opportunity to create a class game. The length of the game is not stated in the product guidelines, so the teacher can determine what works best. It may be a good idea to have students start with shorter games and work up to longer games with a review focus.

Time Frame

- 2–3 weeks—Students are given the menus as the unit is started. As the teacher presents lessons throughout the week, he or she should refer back to the menu options associated with that content. The teacher will go over all of the options for that content and have students place check marks in the boxes that represent the activities they are most interested in completing. If students are using the Tic-Tac-Toe menu form, activities chosen and completed should make a column or row. If students are using the Meal menu form, students will complete one product from each meal, with dessert being an optional enrichment product. When students complete these patterns, they will have completed one activity from each content area, learning style, or level of Bloom's Revised taxonomy.
- 1 week—At the start of the unit, the teacher chooses the three activities he or she feels are most valuable for students. Stations can be set up in the classroom. These three activities are available for student choice throughout the week as regular instruction takes place.
- 1–2 days—The teacher chooses an activity from the menu to use with the entire class.

Suggested Forms

- All-purpose rubric
- Free-choice proposal form

Problem Solving

Directions: Choose one activity each for breakfast, lunch, and dinner. Dessert is an activity you can choose to do after you have finished your other meals. All products must be completed by: _____.

Breakfast

☐ Create a set of trading cards for the various problem-solving strategies. Include a real-world example on each card.

☐ Create a song or rap that teaches the different problem-solving strategies. Teach it to your classmates!

☐ Create a poster with each of the different problem-solving strategies you have used in the past. Include examples of each in your display.

Lunch

☐ Develop a brochure that explains the different problem-solving strategies and how a student could decide which strategy to use.

☐ Which problem-solving technique do you find the most helpful? Create an advertisement for this technique and include specific reasons why you feel that strategy is the best.

☐ Select three different word problems and create a PowerPoint presentation that shows the best way to solve each one.

Dinner

☐ Create a set of concentration cards that focuses not on the correct answer to word problems, but rather on whether an answer is reasonable.

☐ Create a folded quiz book with at least three different word problems, each with one reasonable answer and one unreasonable answer. The purpose of your quiz is not to calculate the correct answer, but to determine which answer is the most reasonable.

☐ Free choice—Submit a free-choice proposal that shares how to use reason to show if an answer could be correct to your teacher for approval.

Dessert

☐ Write a children's book that presents a multiple-step word problem and solves it through a story.

☐ Create a problem-solving puppet that likes to teach others about different problem-solving methods.

Problem Solving

Directions: Check the boxes you plan to complete. They should form a tic-tac-toe across or down. All products are due by: _____.

☐ *Evaluating Problem-Solving Strategies* Develop a brochure that explains the different problem-solving strategies and how a student could decide which strategy to use.	☐ *Evaluating Reasonableness* Write a children's book about Mr. Unreasonable, who used to solve problems incorrectly with unreasonable answers, but who is now a better problem solver.	☐ *Using Problem Solving* Create a set of trading cards for the various problem-solving strategies. Include a real-world example on each card.
☐ *Using Problem Solving* Create a song or rap that teaches the different problem-solving strategies. Teach it to your classmates!	☐ **Free Choice: Evaluating Problem-Solving Strategies** (Fill out your proposal form before beginning the free choice!)	☐ *Evaluating Reasonableness* Create a folded quiz book with at least five different word problems, each with one reasonable answer and one unreasonable answer. The purpose of your quiz is not to calculate the correct answer, but to determine which answer is the most reasonable.
☐ *Evaluating Reasonableness* Create a class game that focuses not on the correct answer to word problems, but rather whether an answer is reasonable.	☐ *Using Problem Solving* Create a bulletin board display for each of the different problem-solving strategies you have used in the past. Include examples of each in your display.	☐ *Evaluating Problem-Solving Strategies* Which problem-solving technique do you find the most helpful? Create an advertisement for this technique and include specific reasons why you feel that strategy is the best.

Fractions and Decimals

List Menus

Objectives Covered Through These Menus and These Activities
- Students will convert between fractions and decimals.
- Students will add, subtract, multiply, and divide fractions and decimals.

Materials Needed by Students for Completion
- Poster board or large white paper
- Socks (for puppets)
- Paper bags (for puppets)
- Ruler (for comic strips)
- Graph paper or Internet access (for crossword puzzles)
- Cookbooks or access to recipes (for recipe cards)
- Blank index cards (for trading cards and concentration cards)
- Materials for board games (e.g., folders, colored cards) ●
- Materials for class games
- Microsoft PowerPoint or other slideshow software
- Materials for quiz boards (e.g., batteries, holiday lights, aluminum foil, tape) ▲

Special Notes on the Use of These Menus
These menus give students the opportunity to create a class game. The length of the game is not stated in the product guidelines, so the teacher can determine what works best. It may be a good idea to have students start with shorter games and work up to longer games with a review focus.

The triangle menu offers students the opportunity to create a quiz board. Quiz boards can range from simple to very complex, depending on the knowledge and ability of the student. Quiz boards work best when the teacher creates a "tester" that can be used to check any boards that are submitted. Basic instructions on how to create quiz boards and testers can be found at http://www.cesiscience.org/attachments/article/100/QuizBoardDirections.pdf.

Time Frame

- 1–2 weeks—Students are given the menus as the unit is started, and guidelines and point expectations are discussed. Students will usually need to earn 100 points for 100%, although there is an opportunity for extra credit if the teacher would like to use another target number. Because these menus cover one topic in depth, the teacher will go over all of the options on the menus and have students place check marks in the boxes next to the activities they are most interested in completing. Teachers will need to set aside a few moments with each student to sign the agreement at the bottom of the page. As instruction continues, activities are completed by students and submitted for grading.
- 1–2 days—The teacher chooses an activity or product from an objective to use with the entire class during lesson time.

Suggested Forms

- All-purpose rubric
- Point-based free-choice proposal form

Name:_____ Date:_____ ▲

Fractions and Decimals: Side 1

Guidelines:

1. You may complete as many of the activities listed as you can within the time period.
2. You may choose any combination of activities.
3. Your goal is 100 points. You may earn up to _____ points extra credit.
4. You may be as creative as you like within the guidelines listed below.
5. You must show your plan to your teacher by _____.
6. Activities may be turned in at any time during the working time period. They will be graded and recorded on this sheet as you continue to work, so keep it safe!

Plan to Do	Activity to Complete (Side 1: 15–25 points)	Point Value	Date Completed	Points Earned
	Complete another student's crossword puzzle.	15		
	Make a how-to brochure that shows the steps for adding and subtracting decimals.	15		
	Create a poster with the decimal equivalents of the most common fractions. Include a drawing of the decimals and fractions.	15		
	Create a set of concentration cards for fractions and their corresponding decimal equivalents.	20		
	Design a quiz board that has users match fraction and decimal word problems with their correct answers.	20		
	Create Three Facts and a Fib about multiplying and dividing fractions.	20		
	Create a Venn diagram that compares and contrasts decimals and fractions.	20		
	Create a pie graph that contains at least five different fractional pieces. Label each piece with its fraction and decimal.	20		
	Design a greeting card that uses fractions in a funny way.	25		
	Create a number crossword puzzle for different fraction and decimal problems.	25		
	Create a comic strip in which the characters have to use decimals in a calculation. The calculation must have at least four steps and end with the number 13.82.	25		
	Create a 6-flap flipbook with decimals on the top flaps. Place at least three equivalent fractions for each decimal inside each flap.	25		
	Total number of points you are planning to earn from Side 1.		**Total points earned from Side 1:**	

Name:_____ Date:_____ ▲

Fractions and Decimals: Side 2

Plan to Do	Activity to Complete (Side 2: 30 points and up)	Point Value	Date Completed	Points Earned
	Create a fraction puppet and use it to explain how to convert fractions to decimals.	30		
	Create a PowerPoint presentation that shows how to add, subtract, multiply, and divide fractions and decimals.	30		
	Create a set of trading cards for all of the decimals in the eighths family. Include their equivalent fractions and at least one drawing.	30		
	Create a song or rap to help your classmates remember the process for adding and subtracting fractions.	30		
	Select a recipe for your favorite food. Create a recipe card for a single serving of this recipe (for one person), and on the back write the recipe for 30 servings.	30		
	Design a class game that allows your classmates to practice their decimal and fraction skills.	35		
	Make a children's book that shows how to complete word problems using fractions and decimals, as well as how to convert between the two. Include examples that would interest your young readers.	35		
	You have decided to open Frantic Fractional, a store that always offers popular items at a fraction of their usual costs. Select at least 20 items and create a windowpane with a picture of each item, its regular cost, the fraction it will be discounted by, and its new cost.	40		
	Write and perform a play about a fraction family that has decided to convert to decimals, hoping the children in their neighborhood will like them better in their new form.	40		
	Free choice: must be outlined on a proposal form and approved before beginning work.	10–40 points		
	Total number of points you are planning to earn from Side 1.	**Total points earned from Side 1:**		
	Total number of points you are planning to earn from Side 2.	**Total points earned from Side 2:**		
		Grand Total (/100)		

I am planning to complete _____ activities that could earn up to a total of _____ points.

Teacher's initials _____ Student's signature _____

Name:_____ Date:_____

Fractions and Decimals: Side 1

Guidelines:

1. You may complete as many of the activities listed as you can within the time period.
2. You may choose any combination of activities.
3. Your goal is 100 points. You may earn up to _____ points extra credit.
4. You may be as creative as you like within the guidelines listed below.
5. You must show your plan to your teacher by _____.
6. Activities may be turned in at any time during the working time period. They will be graded and recorded on this sheet as you continue to work, so keep it safe!

Plan to Do	Activity to Complete (Side 1: 10–25 points)	Point Value	Date Completed	Points Earned
	Complete another student's crossword puzzle.	10		
	Create a pie graph containing at least eight different fractional pieces. Label each piece's fraction and decimal.	15		
	Create a poster with the decimal equivalents of the most common fractions. Include a drawing of the decimals and fractions.	15		
	Create a set of concentration cards for fractions and their corresponding decimal equivalents.	15		
	Create a 10-flap flipbook with decimals on the top flaps. Place at least three equivalent fractions for each decimal inside each flap.	20		
	Create a comic strip in which the characters use decimals in a calculation that has at least five steps and ends with the number 13.82.	20		
	Create a Venn diagram that compares and contrasts decimals and fractions.	20		
	Design a funny greeting card that uses fractions.	20		
	Create Three Facts and a Fib about multiplying and dividing fractions.	20		
	Create a number crossword puzzle for different fraction and decimal problems.	25		
	Create a PowerPoint presentation that shows how to add, subtract, multiply, and divide fractions and decimals.	25		
	Create a set of trading cards for all of the decimals in the eighths family. Include their equivalent fractions, facts about them, and at least one drawing.	25		
	Create a recipe card for a single serving of your favorite food (for one person), and on the back write a recipe for 50 servings.	25		
Total number of points you are planning to earn from Side 1.		**Total points earned from Side 1:**		

Name:_____ Date:_____ ●

Fractions and Decimals: Side 2

Plan to Do	Activity to Complete (Side 2: 30 points and up)	Point Value	Date Completed	Points Earned
	Create a fraction puppet and use it to explain how to convert fractions to decimals.	30		
	Create a song or rap to help your classmates remember the process for adding and subtracting fractions.	30		
	Create a board game in which players answer questions and complete calculations for fractions and decimals.	30		
	Design a class game that allows your classmates to practice their decimal and fraction skills.	30		
	Make a children's book that shows how to complete word problems using fractions and decimals, as well as how to convert between the two. Include examples that would interest your young readers.	30		
	You have decided to open Frantic Fractional, a store that offers popular items at a fraction of their actual costs. Select at least 20 items and create a windowpane with a picture of each item, its regular cost, the fraction it will be discounted by, and its new cost.	30		
	Write and perform a play about a fraction family that has decided to convert to decimals, hoping the children in their neighborhood will like them better in their new form.	35		
	Free choice: must be outlined on a proposal form and approved before beginning work.	10–40 points		
	Total number of points you are planning to earn from Side 1.	**Total points earned from Side 1:**		
	Total number of points you are planning to earn from Side 2.	**Total points earned from Side 2:**		
		Grand Total (/100)		

I am planning to complete _____ activities that could earn up to a total of _____ points.

Teacher's initials _____ Student's signature _____

```
20
 ☐ _____
50
 ☐ _____
 ☐ _____
 ☐ _____
 ☐ _____
80
 ☐ _____
 ☐ _____
```

Adding and Subtracting Fractions

20-50-80 Menus

Objectives Covered Through These Menus and These Activities

- Students will complete word problems that require addition and subtraction of fractions, including mixed numbers and improper fractions.
- Students will recognize real-world applications of the addition and subtraction of fractions.

Materials Needed by Students for Completion

- Poster board or large white paper
- Materials for board games (e.g., folders, colored cards)
- Manipulatives and other materials for models ●
- Materials for student-designed cooking shows
- DVD or VHS recorder (for cooking show videos)
- Magazines (for collages)

Special Notes on the Use of These Menus

These menus give students the opportunity to create a cooking show. Some students may want to perform their show live, whereas others may want to record their show instead. The teacher can give students both options and allow them to choose what works best.

Time Frame

- 1–2 weeks—Students are given the menus as the unit is started, and the teacher discusses all of the product options on the menus. As the different options are discussed, students will choose products that add to a total of 100 points. As the lessons progress, the teacher and students refer back to the menu options associated with the content being taught.
- 1–2 days—The teacher chooses an activity or product from the menu to use with the entire class.

Suggested Forms

- All-purpose rubric
- Student-taught lesson rubric (can be used for cooking show)
- Point-based free-choice proposal form

Adding and Subtracting Fractions

Directions: Choose at least two activities from the menu below. The activities must total at least 100 points. Place a check mark next to each box to show which activities you will complete. All activities must be completed by: _____.

20 Points

❑ Create a windowpane that shows at least six examples of adding and subtracting improper fractions and mixed numbers. Be sure to show each step!

❑ Create a brochure that provides instructions for adding and subtracting improper fractions and mixed numbers.

50 Points

❑ Make a fraction board game that tests your classmates' knowledge of adding and subtracting fractions using real-world word problems.

❑ Design a worksheet that shows a step-by-step example of how to add and subtract fractions. Include mixed numbers and improper fractions, as well as at least 10 practice problems for your classmates.

❑ Make a collage with at least 10 real-world examples of mixed numbers and improper fractions. Use your collage to create eight word problems, and answer each problem.

❑ Free choice—Prepare a proposal form and submit your idea for approval.

80 Points

❑ Write a children's book about the number 12 and its job as a popular and busy common denominator used by many mixed and improper fractions.

❑ Create your own cooking show video in which you prepare a food item for the audience. Your assistants did not bring enough materials and have only provided you with a 1/2-cup measuring cup and a 1/2-teaspoon measure in order to make your recipe. As you prepare your dish for your audience, be sure to explain how you can make your measurements using these smaller measuring tools.

Adding and Subtracting Fractions

Directions: Choose at least two activities from the menu below. The activities must total at least 100 points. Place a check mark next to each box to show which activities you will complete. All activities must be completed by: _____.

---

20 Points

❐ Design a worksheet that shows a step-by-step example of how to add and subtract fractions. Include mixed numbers and improper fractions, as well as at least 15 practice problems for your classmates.

❐ Create a brochure that provides instructions for adding and subtracting improper fractions and mixed numbers.

---

50 Points

❐ Make a fraction board game that tests your classmates' knowledge of adding and subtracting fractions using real-world word problems.

❐ Students often have trouble when completing a fraction subtraction problem that requires borrowing. Create a model that uses manipulatives to help students better understand the process of borrowing.

❐ Make a collage with at least 15 real-world examples of mixed numbers and improper fractions. Use your collage to create 10 word problems, and answer each problem.

❐ Free choice—Prepare a proposal form and submit your idea for approval.

---

80 Points

❐ Create your own cooking show video in which you prepare a food item for the audience. Your assistants did not bring enough materials and have only provided you with a 1/4-cup measuring cup and a 1/2-teaspoon measure in order to make your recipe. As you prepare your dish for the audience, be sure to explain how you can make your measurements using these smaller measuring tools.

❐ Write a children's book about the number 24 and its job as a popular and busy common denominator used by many mixed and improper fractions.

```
20
  ❑ _____
  ❑ _____
50
  ❑ _____
  ❑ _____
  ❑ _____
  ❑ _____
80
  ❑ _____
  ❑ _____
```

Integers

20-50-80 Menus

Objective Covered Through These Menus and These Activities

- Students will identify real-world examples of addition, subtraction, multiplication, and division of integers.

Materials Needed by Students for Completion

- Poster board or large white paper
- Scrapbooking materials ●
- Newspapers (for posters and scrapbooks)
- Magazines (for collages)
- Microsoft PowerPoint or other slideshow software

Time Frame

- 1–2 weeks—Students are given the menus as the unit is started, and the teacher discusses all of the product options on the menus. As the different options are discussed, students will choose products that add to a total of 100 points. As the lessons progress, the teacher and students refer back to the menu options associated with the content being taught.
- 1–2 days—The teacher chooses an activity or product from the menu to use with the entire class.

Suggested Forms

- All-purpose rubric
- Point-based free-choice proposal forms

Integers

Directions: Choose at least two activities from the menu below. The activities must total at least 100 points. Place a check mark next to each box to show which activities you will complete. All activities must be completed by: _____.

---

20 Points

- ❑ Create a PowerPoint presentation that has examples of adding, subtracting, multiplying, and dividing integers; however, use only pictures for your problems.

- ❑ Design a windowpane that shows pictorial examples of all of the different types of integer problems.

---

50 Points

- ❑ Create an integer song or rap that can help students remember how the signs of integers change in different types of problems.

- ❑ Create a brochure that shows how to complete calculations with integers. Be sure to include examples of word problems readers might encounter!

- ❑ Using the newspaper, locate an article that can be used to create three integer word problems. Create a poster to show your article, the word problems, and the solutions. Be sure to include addition, subtraction, multiplication, and division, as well as positive and negative integers.

- ❑ Free choice—Prepare a proposal form and submit your idea for approval.

---

80 Points

- ❑ Create a collage for the number 24 with at least 10 different integer calculations, including addition, subtraction, multiplication, and division, that have 36 as their answer. Be creative in your integer equations; try not to make them sequential.

- ❑ The idea that two negatives do not make a positive is not always true in mathematics. After investigating the interaction of integers, design a children's book that shows how they interact differently depending on the type of problem.

Name:_____ Date:_____

Integers

Directions: Choose at least two activities from the menu below. The activities must total at least 100 points. Place a check mark next to each box to show which activities you will complete. All activities must be completed by: _____.

20 Points

❏ Create an integer song or rap that can help students remember how the signs of integers change in different types of problems.

❏ Design a poster that shows pictorial examples of all of the different types of integer problems.

50 Points

❏ Create a brochure that shows how to complete calculations with integers. Be sure to include examples of word problems readers might encounter!

❏ Create two Three Facts and a Fibs. One should be about adding and subtracting integers, and the other about multiplying and dividing them.

❏ The idea that two negatives do not make a positive is not always true in mathematics. After investigating the interaction of integers, design a PowerPoint presentation to show how they interact differently depending on the type of problem.

❏ Free choice—Prepare a proposal form and submit your idea for approval.

80 Points

❏ Create a collage for the number 36 with at least 25 different integer calculations, including addition, subtraction, multiplication, and division, that have 36 as their answer. Be creative in your integer equations; try not to make them sequential.

❏ Using the newspaper, locate at least two articles that can be used to create four integer word problems. Create a scrapbook to show the articles, the word problems, and the solutions. Be sure to include addition, subtraction, multiplication, and division, as well as positive and negative integers.

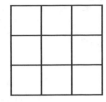

Order of Operations

Meal Menu ▲ and Tic-Tac-Toe Menu ●

Objectives Covered Through These Menus and These Activities

• Students will explain to others how to use the acronym PEMDAS (parentheses, exponents, multiplication, division, addition, and subtraction) when solving order of operations problems.

• Students will brainstorm and solve multistep problems that require the use of order of operations.

Materials Needed by Students for Completion

• Poster board or large white paper
• Graph paper or Internet access (for crossword puzzles) ▲
• Dice or product cube template for class games
• Coat hangers (for mobiles)
• Blank index cards (for mobiles)
• String (for mobiles)

Special Notes on the Use of These menus

This topic has two different menu formats: Meal menu and Tic-Tac-Toe menu. The Meal menu is specifically selected for its meal-oriented, Bloom's-based options, as it is easily broken into manageable bits. The menu can be cut into strips, each strip featuring its own meal, to be given to students. This way, once students have chosen and submitted the breakfast product for grading, they can move on to the lunch strip, and lastly, they can complete the dinner and dessert strips. Because this type of menu is designed to become more advanced as students move through the meals, teachers may choose to provide their students who have special needs with just the meals and save the dessert for enrichment.

These menus give students the opportunity to create a class game. The length of the game is not stated in the product guidelines, so the teacher can determine what works best. It may be a good idea to have students start with shorter games and work up to longer games with a review focus.

Time Frame

- 2–3 weeks—Students are given the menus as the unit is started. As the teacher presents lessons throughout the week, he or she should refer back to the menu options associated with that content. The teacher will go over all of the options for that content and have students place check marks in the boxes that represent the activities they are most interested in completing. If students are using the Tic-Tac-Toe menu form, activities chosen and completed should make a column or row. If students are using the Meal menu form, students will complete one product from each meal, with dessert being an optional enrichment product. When students complete these patterns, they will have completed one activity from each content area, learning style, or level of Bloom's Revised taxonomy.

- 1 week—At the start of the unit, the teacher chooses the three activities he or she feels are most valuable for students. Stations can be set up in the classroom. These three activities are available for student choice throughout the week as regular instruction takes place.

- 1–2 days—The teacher chooses an activity from the menu to use with the entire class.

Suggested Forms

- All-purpose rubric
- Student-taught lesson rubric
- Free-choice proposal form

Order of Operations

Directions: Choose one activity each for breakfast, lunch, and dinner. Dessert is an activity you can choose to do after you have finished your other meals. All products must be completed by: _____.

Breakfast

❒ Rewrite the "Hokey Pokey" song to teach the order of operations to your classmates. Be ready to get up and have the class dance with you as you complete a problem of your choice!

❒ Develop three ways to remember the order of operations. Survey your classmates to decide which one is the most helpful. Create a poster to share your ideas and the best way to remember the order of operations based on the survey results.

❒ Free choice—Submit a proposal form about remembering the steps in the order of operations to your teacher for approval.

Lunch

❒ Your age is your goal number. Create Three Facts and a Fib for your target number using order of operations. The operation statements must include all of the PEMDAS statements and at least three different calculations.

❒ Choose a prime number between 11 and 23. Create a mobile for your number that includes multiple complex methods of obtaining your target number.

❒ You have been given the goal number of 8. Brainstorm at least eight different operation sequences using all of the functions of PEMDAS to achieve your goal number. Use a poster to show the different ways you achieved your goal.

Dinner

❒ Create a children's book that makes the order of operations fun, understandable, and applicable to students' real lives. Include at least two creative problems in your book.

❒ Create an order of operations brochure that explains how to solve complex multiple-step order of operations problems. Include various examples to illustrate your explanation.

❒ Create an order of operations number crossword puzzle. Each clue should include at least three different operations. Be sure to double check your answers!

Dessert

❒ Create a class game that uses a cube or dice to test players' understanding of the order of operations using real-world situations and problems.

❒ Perform a play in which an incorrect order of operations calculation creates a funny situation.

Name:_____ Date:_____

Order of Operations

Directions: Check the boxes you plan to complete. They should form a tic-tac-toe across or down. All products are due by: _____.

☐ *Please Excuse Who?* Rewrite the "Hokey Pokey" song to teach the order of operations to your classmates. Be ready to get up and have the class dance with you as you complete a problem of your choice!	☐ *It's as Easy as 1, 2, 3!* Create a class game that uses cubes or dice to test players' understanding of the order of operations using real-world situations and problems.	☐ *Know Your Goal!* Choose any prime number greater than 11. Create a mobile for your number that includes multiple complex methods of obtaining your target number.
☐ *Know Your Goal!* You have been given the goal number of 5. Brainstorm at least 10 different operation sequences using all of the functions of PEMDAS to achieve your goal number. Use a poster to show the different ways you achieved your goal.	☐ **Free Choice: Teaching PEMDAS** (Fill out your proposal form before beginning the free choice!)	☐ *It's as Easy as 1, 2, 3!* Create a children's book that makes the order of operations fun, understandable, and applicable to students' real lives. Include at least two creative problems in your book.
☐ *It's as Easy as 1, 2, 3!* Create an order of operations brochure that explains how to solve complex multiple-step order of operations problems. Include various examples to illustrate your explanation.	☐ *Know Your Goal!* Your age is your goal number. Create Three Facts and a Fib for your target number using order of operations. The operation statements must include all of the PEMDAS statements and at least five different calculations.	☐ *Please Excuse Who?* Create a short class lesson that teaches students alternate ways to remember the order of operations. Allow plenty of practice on both simple and complex examples.

Mean, Median, Mode, and Range

List Menus

Objectives Covered Through These Menus and These Activities
- Students will identify real-world examples of mean, median, mode, and range.
- Students will calculate mean, median, mode, and range for given or obtained sets of data.

Materials Needed by Students for Completion
- Poster board or large white paper
- Newspapers (for scrapbooks and Three Facts and a Fibs)
- Magazines (for collages)
- Materials for models
- Scrapbooking materials
- Blank index cards (for mobiles)
- Coat hangers (for mobiles)
- String (for mobiles)
- Microsoft PowerPoint or other slideshow software
- Internet access (for WebQuests)
- Materials for board games (e.g., folders, colored cards)

Special Notes on the Use of These Menus
These menus allow students to create a WebQuest. There are multiple versions and templates for WebQuests available on the Internet. Teachers should decide whether to specify a certain format or allow students to create one of their own choosing.

Time Frame
- 1–2 weeks—Students are given the menus as the unit is started, and guidelines and point expectations are discussed. Students will usually need to earn 100 points for 100%, although there is an opportunity for extra credit if the teacher would like to use another target number. Because these menus cover one topic in depth, the teacher will go over all of the options on the menus and have students place check marks in the boxes next to the activities they are most interested in

completing. Teachers will need to set aside a few moments with each student to sign the agreement at the bottom of the page. As instruction continues, activities are completed by students and submitted for grading.

- 1–2 days—The teacher chooses an activity or product from an objective to use with the entire class during lesson time.

Suggested Forms

- All-purpose rubric
- Free-choice proposal form for point-based products

Mean, Median, Mode, and Range: Side 1

Guidelines:

1. You may complete as many of the activities listed as you can within the time period.
2. You may choose any combination of activities.
3. Your goal is 100 points. You may earn up to _____ points extra credit.
4. You may be as creative as you like within the guidelines listed below.
5. You must show your plan to your teacher by _____.
6. Activities may be turned in at any time during the working time period. They will be graded and recorded on this sheet as you continue to work, so keep it safe!

Plan to Do	Activity to Complete (Side 1: 15–30 points)	Point Value	Date Completed	Points Earned
	Create a windowpane for the key statistical concepts we are discussing.	15		
	Make a statistics mobile that shares a set of data you have collected in one of your classes. Then include the mean, median, mode, and range for those data.	15		
	Make a Venn diagram to compare and contrast mean and mode.	15		
	Create a flipbook for mean, median, mode, and range. Share an example of each and explain how to calculate each one.	20		
	Make a model that could be used to show the mean, median, mode, and range of a set of data.	20		
	Create a worksheet with real-world examples and problems for mean, mode, and range.	20		
	Make a collage of pictures and then develop at least five questions about the mean and mode of the pictures you selected.	25		
	Select a chart or data set from the newspaper and create Three Facts and a Fib about the data's mean, median, and range.	25		
	Create a board game for mean, median, mode, and range. Focus on real-world applications of each and how to calculate all four.	30		
	Create a scrapbook of newspaper articles with real-world examples of mean, median, mode, and range. Discuss each article and what it shares. These exact words do not have to be mentioned in the article.	30		
	Write and perform a song or rap to help your classmates remember the difference between mean, median, and mode.	30		
	Total number of points you are planning to earn from Side 1.		**Total points earned from Side 1:**	

Mean, Median, Mode, and Range: Side 2

Plan to Do	Activity to Complete (Side 2: 35 points and up)	Point Value	Date Completed	Points Earned
	Are you the mean, median, or mode in your classroom? Choose one physical aspect of your classmates (e.g., height, diameter of head) and, after recording the data in a table, calculate and show the mean, median, and mode.	35		
	Consider the career you wish to pursue when you graduate from college. Research the various salaries of this profession based on experience and time in the field. Create a poster that shows your research. After determining the mean, median, mode, and range for the salaries, explain which method of calculation you would prefer to determine your starting salary.	35		
	Create a questionnaire to gather data about three questions about a popular topic, and have at least eight people complete it. Present the mean, median, and mode of your data.	35		
	Using the sports section of the newspaper, research the statistics of at least eight players of one sport. After gathering the data, record the mean, median, and mode for the players on either a poster or PowerPoint presentation. Explain what each number means to the sport.	35		
	Choose a company and use the Internet to research the mean, median, mode, and range of its stocks of the past 52-week period. Create a PowerPoint presentation that shares the information in the most positive light. Present it to the class.	40		
	Design a WebQuest that visits various sites that contain data. Have your classmates complete the WebQuest and use the data in a meaningful way to calculate means, modes, and ranges.	40		
	Free choice: must be outlined on a proposal form and approved before beginning work.	10–40 points		
	Total number of points you are planning to earn from Side 1.	**Total points earned from Side 1:**		
	Total number of points you are planning to earn from Side 2.	**Total points earned from Side 2:**		
		Grand Total (/100)		

I am planning to complete _____ activities that could earn up to a total of _____ points.

Teacher's initials _____ Student's signature _____

Name:_____ Date:_____

Mean, Median, Mode, and Range: Side 1

Guidelines:

1. You may complete as many of the activities listed as you can within the time period.
2. You may choose any combination of activities.
3. Your goal is 100 points. You may earn up to _____ points extra credit.
4. You may be as creative as you like within the guidelines listed below.
5. You must show your plan to your teacher by _____.
6. Activities may be turned in at any time during the working time period. They will be graded and recorded on this sheet as you continue to work, so keep it safe!

Plan to Do	Activity to Complete (Side 1: 15–25 points)	Point Value	Date Completed	Points Earned
	Create a flipbook for mean, median, mode, and range. Share an example of each and how to calculate each one.	15		
	Create a windowpane for the key statistical concepts we are discussing.	15		
	Make a model that could be used to show the mean, median, mode, and range of a set of data.	15		
	Make a Venn diagram to compare and contrast mean and mode.	15		
	Make a statistics mobile that shares a set of data you have collected in one of your classes. Then include the data's mean, median, mode, and range.	15		
	Make a collage of pictures, and then develop at least seven questions about the mean and mode of the pictures you selected.	20		
	Select a chart or data set from the newspaper and create Three Facts and a Fib about the data's mean, median, and range.	20		
	Create a worksheet with real-world examples and problems for mean, mode, and range.	20		
	Create a scrapbook of newspaper articles with real-world examples of mean, median, mode, and range. Discuss each article and what it shares. These exact words do not have to be mentioned in the article.	25		
	Write and perform a song or rap to help your classmates remember the difference between mean, median, and mode.	25		
	Total number of points you are planning to earn from Side 1.	**Total points earned from Side 1:**		

Name:_____ Date:_____

Mean, Median, Mode, and Range: Side 2

Plan to Do	Activity to Complete (Side 2: 30 points and up)	Point Value	Date Completed	Points Earned
	Are you the mean, median, or mode in your classroom? Choose one physical aspect of your classmates (e.g., height, diameter of head) and, after recording the data in a table, calculate and show the mean, median, and mode.	30		
	Create a board game for mean, median, mode, and range. Focus on real-world applications of each and how to calculate all four.	30		
	Create a questionnaire to gather data about three questions about a popular topic, and have at least 10 people complete it. Present the mean, median, and mode of your data.	30		
	Choose a company and use the Internet to research the mean, median, mode, and range of its stocks for the past 52-week period. Create a PowerPoint presentation that shares the information in the most positive light. Present it to the class.	35		
	Consider the career you wish to pursue when you graduate from college. Research the various salaries of this profession based on experience and time in the field. Create a poster that shows your research. After determining the mean, median, mode, and range for the salaries, share which method of calculation you would prefer to determine your starting salary.	35		
	Design a WebQuest that visits various sites that contain data. Have your classmates complete the WebQuest and use the data in a meaningful way to calculate means, modes, and ranges.	35		
	Using the sports section of the newspaper, research the statistics of at least 15 players of one sport. After gathering the data, record the mean, median, and mode for the players on either a poster or PowerPoint presentation. Explain what each number means.	35		
	Free choice: must be outlined on a proposal form and approved before beginning work.	10–35 points		
	Total number of points you are planning to earn from Side 1.		**Total points earned from Side 1:**	
	Total number of points you are planning to earn from Side 2.		**Total points earned from Side 2:**	
			Grand Total (/100)	

I am planning to complete _____ activities that could earn up to a total of _____ points.

Teacher's initials _____ Student's signature _____

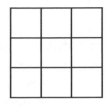

Ratios

Meal Menu ▲ and Tic-Tac-Toe Menu ●

Objectives Covered Through These Menus and These Activities
- Students will use ratios to describe proportional situations.
- Students will represent ratios with models, fractions, and decimals.
- Students will use ratios to make predictions in proportional situations.

Materials Needed by Students for Completion
- Poster board or large white paper
- Blank index cards (for concentration cards and trading cards)
- Newspapers and magazines (for collages)
- Materials for bulletin board display
- Microsoft PowerPoint or other slideshow software ▲
- Materials for board games (e.g., folders, colored cards) ●
- Three-dimensional timeline materials
- Scrapbooking materials ▲
- DVD or VHS recorder (for videos)

Special Notes on the Use of These Menus
This topic has two different menu formats: Meal menu and Tic-Tac-Toe menu. The Meal menu is specifically selected for its meal-oriented, Bloom's-based options, as it is easily broken into manageable bits. The menu can be cut into strips, each strip featuring its own meal, to be given to students. This way, once students have chosen and submitted the breakfast product for grading, they can move on to the lunch strip, and lastly, they can complete the dinner and dessert strips. Because this type of menu is designed to become more advanced as students move through the meals, teachers may choose to provide their students who have special needs with just the meals and save the dessert for enrichment.

These menus allow students to create a bulletin board display. Some classrooms may only have one bulletin board, so the teacher can divide the board into sections, or additional classroom wall or hall space can be sectioned off for the creation of these displays. Students can plan their displays based on the amount of space they are assigned.

These menus give students the opportunity to create a video. Although students enjoy producing their own videos, there are often difficulties obtaining the equipment and scheduling the use of the video recorder. The menus can be modified by allowing students to act out their videos (like a play), or if students have the technology, they may wish to produce a webcam or Flash version of their videos.

Time Frame

- 2–3 weeks—Students are given the menus as the unit is started. As the teacher presents lessons throughout the week, he or she should refer back to the menu options associated with that content. The teacher will go over all of the options for that content and have students place check marks in the boxes that represent the activities they are most interested in completing. If students are using the Tic-Tac-Toe menu form, activities chosen and completed should make a column or row. If students are using the Meal menu form, students will complete one product from each meal, with dessert being an optional enrichment product. When students complete these patterns, they will have completed one activity from each content area, learning style, or level of Bloom's Revised taxonomy.
- 1 week—At the start of the unit, the teacher chooses the three activities he or she feels are most valuable for students. Stations can be set up in the classroom. These three activities are available for student choice throughout the week as regular instruction takes place.
- 1–2 days—The teacher chooses an activity from the menu to use with the entire class.

Suggested Forms

- All-purpose rubric
- Free-choice proposal form

Ratios

Directions: Choose one activity each for breakfast, lunch, and dinner. Dessert is an activity you can choose to do after you have finished your other meals. All products must be completed by: _____.

Breakfast

❑ Create a set of concentration cards that asks students to find matching ratios, fractions, and decimals.

❑ Search through newspapers and magazines to find examples of objects that can be expressed as ratios, fractions, or decimals. Create a collage of the different examples. Write three numbers represented by each one: ratio, fraction, and decimal.

❑ Design a set of trading cards for 10 fractions. Include a real-world example of the fraction, its decimal, and the ratio.

Lunch

❑ Create a scrapbook of ratios that can be found in our daily lives. Be creative in what you choose as examples.

❑ Research how ratios are used to create smaller models of larger objects. Create a PowerPoint presentation that shares at least 10 different examples of scale models and their original object.

❑ Make a three-dimensional timeline for an important time in history. Measure your timeline and use what you know about ratios to place your dates on the timeline.

Dinner

❑ Create a survey to gather information about a recent controversial topic in the news. After surveying eight people, use this information to predict how a larger sample size might respond. Create a speech to share your prediction.

❑ Ratios are often used in the study of heredity to predict the traits of offspring. Research these different types of ratios and create a bulletin board display to share what each ratio predicts and how it is calculated. Include at least three examples with parents and offspring!

❑ Free choice—Submit a free-choice proposal about using ratios to predict something to your teacher for approval.

Dessert

❑ You have been hired by a local public television station to document the exciting lives of ratios in your school and community. Although ratios are all around us, many go unnoticed. Prepare your video to showcase these hidden ratios.

❑ Choose your favorite professional sports team (or athlete) and research its statistics. Prepare a poster about the statistics and their meanings. Include a precise prediction about the team's or athlete's performance in the next game.

Ratios

Directions: Check the boxes you plan to complete. They should form a tic-tac-toe across or down. All products are due by: _____.

☐ *Everyday Ratios* You have been hired by a local public television station to document the exciting lives of ratios in your school and community. Although ratios are all around us, many go unnoticed. Prepare a video to showcase these hidden ratios.	☐ *Can Ratios Predict the Future?* Create a survey to gather information about a recent controversial topic in the news. After surveying 10 people, use this information to predict how a larger sample size might respond. Create a speech to share your prediction.	☐ *Ratios, Fractions, and Decimals, Oh My!* Create a set of concentration cards that asks students to find matching ratios, fractions, and decimals.
☐ *Ratios, Fractions, and Decimals, Oh My!* Search through newspapers and magazines to find examples of objects that can be expressed as ratios, fractions, or decimals. Create a collage of the different examples. Write three numbers represented by each one: ratio, fraction, and decimal.	☐ **Free Choice: Everyday Ratios** (Fill out your proposal form before beginning the free choice!)	☐ *Can Ratios Predict the Future?* Ratios are often used in the study of heredity to predict the traits of offspring. Research these different types of ratios and create a bulletin board display to share what each ratio predicts and how it is calculated. Include at least five examples with parents and offspring!
☐ *Can Ratios Predict the Future?* Choose your favorite professional team (or athlete) and research its statistics. Prepare a poster about the statistics and their meanings. Include a precise prediction about the team's or athlete's performance in the next game.	☐ *Ratios, Fractions, and Decimals, Oh My!* Design a board game for practicing the conversions between ratios, fractions, and decimals. Include an answer key so players can double check their responses.	☐ *Everyday Ratios* Make a three-dimensional timeline for an important time in history. Measure your timeline and use what you know about ratios to place your dates on the timeline.

CHAPTER 6

Geometry

```
20
  ❑ ____
  ❑ ____
50
  ❑ ____
  ❑ ____
  ❑ ____
80
  ❑ ____
  ❑ ____
```

Angles

20-50-80 Menus

Objectives Covered Through These Menus and These Activities
- Students will use angle measurements to classify angles as acute, obtuse, or right.
- Students will classify angle pairs as complementary or supplementary.

Materials Needed by Students for Completion
- Poster board or large white paper
- Protractors (for mobiles, PowerPoint presentations, free-choice options, and concentration cards)
- Compasses (for student-taught lessons) ●
- Magazines (for collages)
- Blank index cards (for trading cards, concentration cards, and mobiles)
- Coat hangers (for mobiles) ▲
- String (for mobiles) ▲
- Microsoft PowerPoint or other slideshow software
- DVD or VHS recorder (for videos)

Special Notes on the Use of These Menus
These menus give students the opportunity to create a video. Although students enjoy producing their own videos, there are often difficulties obtaining the equipment and scheduling the use of the video recorder. The menus can be modified by allowing students to act out their videos (like a play), or if students have the technology, they may wish to produce a webcam or Flash version of their videos.

Time Frame
- 1–2 weeks—Students are given the menus as the unit is started, and the teacher discusses all of the product options on the menus. As the different options are discussed, students will choose products that add to a total of 100 points. As the lessons progress, the teacher and students refer back to the menu options associated with the content being taught.

- 1–2 days—The teacher chooses an activity or product from the menu to use with the entire class.

Suggested Forms

- All-purpose rubric
- Student-taught lesson rubric
- Point-based free-choice proposal form

Angles

Directions: Choose at least two activities from the menu below. The activities must total at least 100 points. Place a check mark next to each box to show which activities you will complete. All activities must be completed by: _____.

20 Points

- ❑ Create a collage of examples of acute, obtuse, and right angles we see all around us. Outline and label the different angles in each picture.

- ❑ Create a set of trading cards for each type of angle, including complementary and supplementary angles. Include examples seen from the real world.

50 Points

- ❑ Make a mobile for acute, obtuse, and right angles with photos of at least two examples of each angle that can be observed on a daily basis. Use a protractor to measure the angles to prove their classification, and share the measurements as part of your mobile.

- ❑ Design a how-to PowerPoint presentation that shows how to classify the different types of angles, including complementary and supplementary angles, using a protractor.

- ❑ Create a song or rap about complementary and supplementary angles and how to identify them.

- ❑ Free choice—Prepare a proposal form in which you are using a protractor to measure different angles and submit your idea for approval.

80 Points

- ❑ A new game show called "It's All About the Angle!" is being produced by a local television station, and it wants a local student to create the game. Design your version of this show using classmates as contestants. Make a video or perform your game show live.

- ❑ Angles are used in many different professions. Research which occupations use angles and give a You Be the Person presentation as someone who uses angles in his or her job. Be prepared to share how their calculations help you in your work.

Angles

Directions: Choose at least two activities from the menu below. The activities must total at least 100 points. Place a check mark next to each box to show which activities you will complete. All activities must be completed by: _____.

---

20 Points

❑ Create a collage of examples of acute, obtuse, and right angles we see all around us. Label the different angles in each picture.

❑ Create a set of trading cards for each type of angle, including complementary and supplementary angles. Examples should contain ones we see on a daily basis.

---

50 Points

❑ Create a set of concentration cards that have players matching drawn angles with their measurements. Make the game challenging by having some angles only a few degrees apart so players need to use a protractor to check their match.

❑ Design a how-to PowerPoint presentation that shows how to classify the different types of angles, including complementary and supplementary angles, using a protractor. Be sure to include how to use a protractor in your presentation.

❑ Angles are used in many different professions. Research which occupations use angles and give a You Be the Person presentation as someone who uses angles in his or her job. Be prepared to share how their calculations help you in your work.

❑ Free choice—Prepare a proposal form in which you are using a protractor to measure different angles and submit your idea for approval.

---

80 Points

❑ A new game show called "It's All About the Angle!" is being produced by a local television station, and it wants a local student to create the game. Design your version of this show using classmates as contestants. Make a video or perform your game show live.

❑ Create a class lesson that shows students how to use a compass to construct each type of angle, as well as how to create an angle's complement or supplement.

Solid Figures

20-50-80 Menus

Objectives Covered Through These Menus and These Activities

- Students will determine properties of pyramids, cones, prisms, and cylinders.
- Students will identify real-world examples of geometric solids.

Materials Needed by Students for Completion

- Poster board or large white paper
- Materials for board games (e.g., folders, colored cards) ●
- Blank index cards (for trading cards and mobiles)
- Coat hangers (for mobiles)
- String (for mobiles)
- Materials for dioramas (e.g., shoe boxes, cards)
- Materials for models
- Scrapbooking materials
- Internet access (for WebQuests) ●
- Solid figures for sculptures
- Microsoft PowerPoint or other slideshow software ▲

Special Notes on the Use of These Menus

The circle menu allows students to create a WebQuest. There are multiple versions and templates for WebQuests available on the Internet. Teachers should decide whether to specify a certain format or allow students to create one of their own choosing.

Time Frame

- 1–2 weeks—Students are given the menus as the unit is started, and the teacher discusses all of the product options on the menus. As the different options are discussed, students will choose products that add to a total of 100 points. As the lessons progress, the teacher and students refer back to the menu options associated with the content being taught.
- 1–2 days—The teacher chooses an activity or product from the menu to use with the entire class.

Suggested Forms

- All-purpose rubric
- Point-based free-choice proposal form

Solid Figures

Directions: Choose at least two activities from the menu below. The activities must total at least 100 points. Place a check mark next to each box to show which activities you will complete. All activities must be completed by: _____.

---

20 Points

❑ Create a set of trading cards for all of the geometric shapes and solids.

❑ After grouping similar geometric solids together, create a mobile for the solids. Include an example of each and its properties.

---

50 Points

❑ Design a geometric shape PowerPoint presentation in which players learn about the properties of different two- and three-dimensional shapes.

❑ Write your own children's book about the different types of solid figures. Include examples that children would understand.

❑ Design a scrapbook with at least eight pictures of different geometric solids that can be found in your neighborhood. Label and tell about the different shapes. Be creative in where you look for your shapes, from signs, to art, to architecture.

❑ Free choice—Prepare a proposal form about geometric figures and submit your idea for approval.

---

80 Points

❑ Create a sculpture using at least two different-sized pyramids, two cones, two prisms, and one cylinder that you can find at home. After creating your sculpture, write a story that tells about the sculpture and its background.

❑ Create a model or diorama of your bedroom using examples from all of the geometric shapes. Create a key that tells the shapes that form each object.

Solid Figures

Directions: Choose at least two activities from the menu below. The activities must total at least 100 points. Place a check mark next to each box to show which activities you will complete. All activities must be completed by: _____.

---

20 Points

❏ Create a set of trading cards for all of the geometric shapes and solids.

❏ After grouping similar geometric solids together, create a mobile for the solids that includes an example of each solid and its properties.

---

50 Points

❏ Design a geometric shape board game in which players learn about the properties of different two- and three-dimensional shapes.

❏ Create a model or diorama of your bedroom using examples from all of the geometric shapes. Create a key that tells the shapes that form each object.

❏ Design a scrapbook with at least 10 pictures of different geometric solids that can be found in your neighborhood. Label and tell about the different shapes. Be creative in where you look for your shapes, from signs, to art, to architecture.

❏ Free choice—Prepare a proposal form about geometric figures and submit your idea for approval.

---

80 Points

❏ Create a sculpture using at least three different-sized pyramids, two cones, three prisms, and one cylinder that you can find at home. After creating your sculpture, write a story that tells about the sculpture and its background.

❏ Design a WebQuest that exposes users to photographs and examples of structures and sculptures created to represent geometric solids. Focus your questions on identifying the solids represented and their properties.

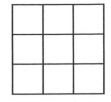

Solids and Spatial Reasoning

Meal Menu ▲ and Tic-Tac-Toe Menu ●

Objectives Covered Through These Menus and These Activities

- Students will sketch solids from various views, including front, back, top, and sides.
- Students will identify pyramids, cones, prisms, and cylinders and their properties.
- Students will show how space figures are used in architectural design.

Materials Needed by Students for Completion

- Poster board or large white paper
- Materials for cross-cut models
- DVD or VHS recorder (for commercials)
- Blank index cards (for mobiles and trading cards)
- Coat hangers (for mobiles) ▲
- String (for mobiles) ▲
- Microsoft PowerPoint or other slideshow software
- Solid figures for sculptures
- Materials for museum exhibits (e.g., boxes, cards)

Special Notes on the Use of These Menus

This topic has two different menu formats: Meal menu and Tic-Tac-Toe menu. The Meal menu is specifically selected for its meal-oriented, Bloom's-based options, as it is easily broken into manageable bits. The menu can be cut into strips, each strip featuring its own meal, to be given to students. This way, once students have chosen and submitted the breakfast product for grading, they can move on to the lunch strip, and lastly, they can complete the dinner and dessert strips. Because this type of menu is designed to become more advanced as students move through the meals, teachers may choose to provide their students who have special needs with just the meals and save the dessert for enrichment.

These menus give students the opportunity to create a commercial. Although students enjoy producing their own videos, there are often difficulties obtaining the equipment and scheduling the use of the video recorder. The menus can be modified by allowing students to act out their videos (like a play), or if students have the technology, they may wish to produce a webcam or Flash version of their videos.

Time Frame

- 2–3 weeks—Students are given the menus as the unit is started. As the teacher presents lessons throughout the week, he or she should refer back to the menu options associated with that content. The teacher will go over all of the options for that content and have students place check marks in the boxes that represent the activities they are most interested in completing. If students are using the Tic-Tac-Toe menu form, activities chosen and completed should make a column or row. If students are using the Meal menu form, students will complete one product from each meal, with dessert being an optional enrichment product. When students complete these patterns, they will have completed one activity from each content area, learning style, or level of Bloom's Revised taxonomy.
- 1 week—At the start of the unit, the teacher chooses the three activities he or she feels are most valuable for students. Stations can be set up in the classroom. These three activities are available for student choice throughout the week as regular instruction takes place.
- 1–2 days—The teacher chooses an activity from the menu to use with the entire class.

Suggested Forms

- All-purpose rubric
- Free-choice proposal form

Solids and Spatial Reasoning

Directions: Choose one activity each for breakfast, lunch, and dinner. Dessert is an activity you can choose to do after you have finished your other meals. All products must be completed by: _____.

Breakfast

❒ Look around your home and find a collection of at least three different examples each of cylinders, pyramids, cones, and prisms (at least 12 examples in total). Label each example with the type of figure it is and bring your collection to school.

❒ Gather at least two examples of different-sized cylinders, pyramids, cones, and prisms. Create a sculpture out of all of the objects. Write a paragraph about your sculpture and the different figures found in it.

❒ Create a mobile for the different solid figures. For each, include the name, a written description, a net for each shape, and a small household example.

Lunch

❒ Create a cross-cut model for each of the different types of solid figures. Include a poster for your figures that also shows all of the exterior views: top, side, front, and back.

❒ Choose two solid figures and make a poster that shows these figures from the front, top, back, and sides.

❒ Design a set of trading cards for all of the solid figures. Each card should discuss the figure as well as show it from the top, side, front, and back.

Dinner

❒ You are an architect, and your client has asked for a home designed only from solid figures. Using only solid figures, create a model of a home for your client. Also include a drawing of the front, sides, and back of the house.

❒ Locate a picture of a castle of your choice and analyze its structure and use of space figures. Create a commercial for your own castle-building business that uses only geometric solids in its designs.

❒ Free choice—Submit a proposal in which you combine solid figures and building to your teacher for approval.

Dessert

❒ Create a "Mystery Figure" PowerPoint presentation in which you show different views of various solid figures from the top, front, side, or back so the audience of the PowerPoint can guess the figure.

❒ The National Geometry Museum is redoing its solid figures exhibit. Create a new exhibit that discusses the different figures, their properties, and examples we see in our daily life.

Name:_____ Date:_____

Solids and Spatial Reasoning

Directions: Check the boxes you plan to complete. They should form a tic-tac-toe across or down. All products are due by: _____.

☐ *Identifying Solid Figures* Look around your home and find a collection of at least four different examples each of cylinders, pyramids, cones, and prisms (at least 16 examples in total). Label each example with the type of figure it is and bring your collection to school.	☐ *Solids From Various Views* Create a cross-cut model for each of the different types of solid figures. Include a poster for your figures that also shows all of the exterior views: top, side, front, and back.	☐ *Solid Figures* Locate a picture of a castle of your choice and analyze its structure and dependence on space figures. Create a commercial for your own castle-building architecture business that uses only geometric solids in its designs.
☐ *Solid Figures* You are an architect, and your client has asked for a home designed from only solid figures. Using only solid figures, create a model of a home for your client. Also include a drawing of the front, sides, and back of the house.	☐ **Free Choice: Identifying Solid Figures** (Fill out your proposal form before beginning the free choice!)	☐ *Solids From Various Views* Design a set of trading cards for all of the solid figures. Each card should discuss the figure as well as show it from the top, side, front, and back.
☐ *Solids From Various Views* Create a "Mystery Figure" PowerPoint presentation in which you show different views of various solid figures from the top, front, side, or back so the audience of the PowerPoint can guess the figure.	☐ *Solid Figures* The National Geometry Museum is redoing its solid figures exhibit. Create a new exhibit that discusses the different figures, their properties, and examples we see in our daily life.	☐ *Identifying Solid Figures* Gather at least three examples of different-sized cylinders, pyramids, cones, and prisms. Create a sculpture out of all of the objects. Write a paragraph about your sculpture and the different figures found in it.

```
20
  □
  □
50
  □
  □
  □
  □
80
  □
  □
```

Circles

20-50-80 Menus

Objectives Covered Through These Menus and These Activities

- Students will calculate the radius, diameter, and circumference of a circle.
- Students will understand the relationship between the measurements of radius and circumference.

Materials Needed by Students for Completion

- Poster board or large white paper
- Magazines (for collages)
- Product cube template ▲
- Microsoft PowerPoint or other slideshow software ●
- Rulers or flexible tape measures to check calculations

Time Frame

- 1–2 weeks—Students are given the menus as the unit is started, and the teacher discusses all of the product options on the menus. As the different options are discussed, students will choose products that add to a total of 100 points. As the lessons progress, the teacher and students refer back to the menu options associated with the content being taught.
- 1–2 days—The teacher chooses an activity or product from the menu to use with the entire class.

Suggested Forms

- All-purpose rubric
- Point-based free-choice proposal form

Circles

Directions: Choose at least two activities from the menu below. The activities must total at least 100 points. Place a check mark next to each box to show which activities you will complete. All activities must be completed by: _____.

---

20 Points

- ❑ Select at least eight circular objects found in your classroom. Measure and calculate the radius and circumference for each object. Make and label a drawing of each object, and record your findings in a windowpane.

- ❑ Create a collage of circular objects. Using a ruler, measure the radius and diameter and calculate the circumference for each. Record your measurements beside each object in your collage.

---

50 Points

- ❑ Create a children's book about circles and the relationships between their properties.

- ❑ Circles have uses in the real world. Create a cube that shows examples of how circles and the measures of their radii (plural of radius) are used in real-world careers.

- ❑ Create a worksheet for your classmates in which you need to know how to calculate the radius, diameter, and circumference of a circle in order to solve at least eight real-world problems.

- ❑ Free choice—Prepare a proposal form and submit your idea for approval.

---

80 Points

- ❑ There is a special relationship between the diameter and the circumference of a circle. Design a measuring activity that allows you to figure out this relationship. You should test at least eight objects to confirm your results.

- ❑ Your teacher would like to buy the largest circular rug available to cover your classroom floor. Rugs are sold by diameter. Make a poster to propose to your teacher the size of rug that should be purchased, and include a drawing of the pattern and colors you think would be best.

Circles

Directions: Choose at least two activities from the menu below. The activities must total at least 100 points. Place a check mark next to each box to show which activities you will complete. All activities must be completed by: _____.

20 Points

❒ Select at least 10 circular objects found in your classroom. Measure and calculate the radius and circumference for each object. Make and label a drawing of each object, and record your findings in a windowpane.

❒ Create a collage of circular objects. Using a ruler, measure the radius and diameter and calculate the circumference for each. Record your measurements beside each object in your collage.

50 Points

❒ Create a children's book about circles and the relationships between their properties.

❒ Circles have uses in many subject areas. Create a PowerPoint presentation that shows at least five examples of how circles and the measures of their radii (plural of radius) are used in each of the other content areas.

❒ Create a worksheet for your classmates in which you need to know how to calculate the radius, diameter, and circumference of a circle in order to solve at least 10 real-world problems.

❒ Free choice—Prepare a proposal form and submit your idea for approval.

80 Points

❒ There is a special relationship between the diameter and the circumference of a circle. Design a measuring activity that allows you to figure out this relationship. You should test at least 10 objects to confirm your results.

❒ Your teacher would like to buy the largest circular rug available to cover your classroom floor. Rugs are sold by diameter. Make a poster to propose to your teacher the size of rug that should be purchased, and include a drawing of the pattern and colors you think would be best.

Circles Cube

Circles have uses in many professions. Record an example of how circles and the measures of their radii (plural of radius) are used in various careers. Place one example on each side of the cube. Use this pattern or create your own cube.

Measuring Shapes

Game Show Menus

Objectives Covered Through These Menus and These Activities

- Students will calculate area, surface area, perimeter, and volume of various geometric shapes.
- Students will identify how changing one dimension can alter an object's perimeter, area, or volume.

Materials Needed by Students for Completion

- Poster board or large white paper
- Rulers and measuring tape
- Coat hangers (for mobiles)
- Blank index cards (for mobiles)
- String (for mobiles)
- Material for models of specific surface areas
- Materials for board games (e.g., folders, colored cards)
- Microsoft PowerPoint or other slideshow software
- Ping pong ball ●
- Tennis ball ▲
- Metersticks

Special Notes on the Use of These Menus

The higher level activities in these menus have students taking measurements in various locations in the school, from the library, to the gym, to the outside of the school building. Although it is a great experience for students to take their metersticks and start measuring these locations, if safety or classroom management is an issue, then students can certainly use a scaled map of the school to calculate the necessary information.

Time Frame

- 2–3 weeks—Students are given the menus as the unit is started, and the guidelines and point expectations are discussed. As lessons are taught throughout the unit, students and the teacher can refer back to the options associated with the topic. The teacher will go over all of the options for the topic being covered and will have students place check marks in the boxes next to the activities they are most interested in completing. As teaching continues throughout the 2–3 weeks, activities are discussed, chosen, and submitted for grading.

- 1 week—At the beginning of the unit, the teacher chooses an activity from each area that he or she feels would be most valuable for students. Stations can be set up in the classroom. These activities are available for student choice throughout the week as regular instruction takes place.
- 1–2 days—The teacher chooses an activity from an objective to use with the entire class during lesson time.

Suggested Forms

- All-purpose rubric
- Student-taught lesson rubric
- Point-based free-choice proposal form

Guidelines for the Measuring Shapes Game Show Menu

- You must choose at least one activity from each topic area.
- You may not do more than two activities in any one topic area for credit. (You are, of course, welcome to do more than two for your own investigation.)
- Grading will be ongoing, so turn in products as you complete them.
- All free-choice proposals must be turned in and approved prior to working on that free-choice product.
- You must earn 100 points for a 100%. You may earn extra credit up to _____ points.
- You must show your teacher your plan for completion by: _____.

Measuring Shapes

Perimeter	Surface Area	Volume	Changes in Dimensions	Points for Each Level
☐ Choose two rooms in your school and measure their perimeters. Present the rooms and your data. (15 pts.)	☐ Create a poster that shows how to find the areas of at least three different shapes. (15 pts.)	☐ Create a mobile with different space figures, the formulas for calculating the surface area of each, and your results from the calculations. (15 pts.)	☐ Create a brochure that shows examples of the different solids and explains how to calculate the volume of each. (15 pts.)	☐ Create a drawing that shares how changing the measure of one side of a figure impacts its perimeter, area, and volume. (10 pts.)	10–15 points
☐ Choose four different locations on your body and measure their perimeters. Use this information to approximate the volume of material within that area of the body. (25 pts.)	☐ Create an advertisement for a product whose area is its main selling point. (25 pts.)	☐ Make a model of an object whose surface area is exactly 92 square centimeters. (25 pts.)	☐ Design a board game that allows players to estimate the volumes of classroom objects and provides an opportunity for them to test their estimates. (25 pts.)	☐ Create a model that shows how volume changes as perimeter changes. (25 pts.)	25 points
☐ Your school is thinking of putting a new fence all the way around the football field. Determine how to calculate the amount of fencing needed, and then complete the calculations. (30 pts.)	☐ You have been given the task of recarpeting your school's library. Develop a plan for how to accomplish this task. After measuring, make a proposal for the amount of carpet needed. (30 pts.)	☐ The amount of mass a boat can carry is directly related to its surface area. Create a class lesson about this phenomenon. Be sure your classmates get to do some calculations! (30 pts.)	☐ Your teacher made the comment that more than 10,000 tennis balls would fit in your classroom. Develop a calculation method to see if he or she is right. After taking some measurements, propose how many tennis balls the classroom would hold. (30 pts.)	☐ Research a geometric monument. Create a PowerPoint presentation with a picture of your monument and its measurements. Show how the dimensions would change if you created a scale model no taller than 12 inches. (30 pts.)	30 points
Free Choice (prior approval) (25–50 pts.)	Free Choice (prior approval) (25–50 pts.)	Free Choice (prior approval) (25–50 pts.)	Free Choice (prior approval) (25–50 pts.)	Free Choice (prior approval) (25–50 pts.)	25–50 points
Total:	Total:	Total:	Total:	Total:	Total Grade:

Measuring Shapes

Perimeter	Area	Surface Area	Volume	Changes in Dimensions	Points for Each Level
☐ Choose three rooms in your school and measure their perimeters. Present the rooms and your data. (15 pts.)	☐ Create a poster that shows how to find the areas of at least three different shapes. (10 pts.)	☐ Create a mobile with different space figures, the formulas for calculating the surface areas of each, and your results from the calculations. (15 pts.)	☐ Create a brochure that shows examples of the different solids and explains how to calculate the volume of each. (10 pts.)	☐ Create a drawing that shares how changing the measure of one side of a figure impacts its perimeter, area, and volume. (10 pts.)	10–15 points
☐ Choose six different locations on your body and measure their perimeters. Use this information to approximate the volume of material within each area of the body. (25 pts.)	☐ Create an advertisement for a product whose area is its main selling point. (20 pts.)	☐ Make a model of an object whose surface area is exactly 172 square centimeters. (25 pts.)	☐ Design a board game that allows players to estimate the volumes of classroom objects and provides an opportunity for them to test their estimates. (25 pts.)	☐ Create a model that shows how volume changes as perimeter changes. (20 pts.)	20–25 points
☐ Your school is thinking of putting a new fence all the way around the outside area, including the fields. Determine how to calculate the amount of fencing needed and then complete the calculations. (30 pts.)	☐ You have been given the task of recarpeting your school's library. Develop a plan for how to accomplish this task. After measuring, make a proposal for the amount of carpet needed and a reasonable cost. (30 pts.)	☐ The amount of mass a boat can carry is directly related to its surface area. Create a class lesson about this phenomenon. Be sure your classmates get to do some calculations! (30 pts.)	☐ Your teacher made the comment that more than 100,000 ping pong balls would fit in the school gym. Develop a calculation method to see if he or she is right. After taking some measurements, propose the number of ping pong balls the gym would hold. (30 pts.)	☐ Research two geometric monuments around the world. Create a PowerPoint presentation with a picture of each and its measurements. Show how the other dimensions would change if you created a scale model no taller than 12 inches. (30 pts.)	25–30 points
Free Choice (prior approval) (25–50 pts.)	**Free Choice** (prior approval) (25–50 pts.)	**Free Choice** (prior approval) (25–50 pts.)	**Free Choice** (prior approval) (25–50 pts.)	**Free Choice** (prior approval) (25–50 pts.)	25–50 points
Total:	**Total:**	**Total:**	**Total:**	**Total:**	Total Grade:

Surface Area

List Menus

Objectives Covered Through These Menus and These Activities
- Students will demonstrate how to calculate the total and lateral surface area of various space figures, including spheres, prisms, and cylinders.
- Students will use nets to show how surface area is created.
- Students will understand the relationship between volume and surface area.

Materials Needed by Students for Completion
- Poster board or large white paper
- DVD or VHS recorder (for videos)
- Large lined index cards (for instruction cards)
- Microsoft PowerPoint or other slideshow software
- Blank index cards (for concentration cards)
- Graph paper (for nets)
- Basketball
- Materials for museum exhibits (e.g., boxes, cards)

Special Notes on the Use of These Menus
These menus give students the opportunity to create a video. Although students enjoy producing their own videos, there are often difficulties obtaining the equipment and scheduling the use of the video recorder. The menus can be modified by allowing students to act out their videos (like a play), or if students have the technology, they may wish to produce a webcam or Flash version of their videos.

Time Frame
- 1–2 weeks—Students are given the menus as the unit is started, and guidelines and point expectations are discussed. Students will usually need to earn 100 points for 100%, although there is an opportunity for extra credit if the teacher would like to use another target number. Because these menus cover one topic in depth, the teacher will go over all of the options on the menus and have students place check marks in the boxes next to the activities they are most interested in

completing. Teachers will need to set aside a few moments with each student to sign the agreement at the bottom of the page. As instruction continues, activities are completed by students and submitted for grading.

- 1–2 days—The teacher chooses an activity or product from an objective to use with the entire class during lesson time.

Suggested Forms

- All-purpose rubric
- Point-based free-choice proposal form

Name:_____ Date:_____

Surface Area: Side 1

Guidelines:
1. You may complete as many of the activities listed as you can within the time period.
2. You may choose any combination of activities.
3. Your goal is 100 points. You may earn up to _____ points extra credit.
4. You may be as creative as you like within the guidelines listed below.
5. You must show your plan to your teacher by _____.
6. Activities may be turned in at any time during the working time period. They will be graded and recorded on this sheet as you continue to work, so keep it safe!

Plan to Do	Activity to Complete (Side 1: 15–25 points)	Point Value	Date Completed	Points Earned
	Create a set of concentration cards for matching the formulas for different space figures with drawings of the figures.	15		
	Make an acrostic for the term "surface area" in which you share what it is and why it is important to know.	15		
	Create a mind map for the different solids and how we measure lateral surface area, total surface area, and volume for each. Be sure to include examples!	20		
	Create an instruction card for calculating lateral or total surface area of a solid for someone who is not sure what solid he or she is looking at or what any of the variables stand for. Be as specific as you can!	20		
	Create Three Facts and a Fib for the surface area of space figures.	20		
	Create a PowerPoint presentation that shows how to calculate the total and lateral surface areas of various space figures.	25		
	Design a worksheet that focuses on situations where lateral or total surface area is calculated.	25		
	Using graph paper, create your own set of nets for various geometric shapes and show how you use them to calculate total surface area.	25		
	Total number of points you are planning to earn from Side 1.	**Total points earned from Side 1:**		

Surface Area: Side 2

Plan to Do	Activity to Complete (Side 2: 35 points and up)	Point Value	Date Completed	Points Earned
	Make a math video that shows viewers examples of different solids that they might find in their homes, the lateral surface areas, and the total surface areas.	35		
	Develop a class lesson that teaches your classmates about the relationship between surface area and the volume of an object.	35		
	Write and illustrate a children's book about a prism and its quest to have its total surface area calculated.	35		
	Your PE teacher has proposed a challenge: Figure out how many dimples are on a basketball. Using your knowledge of scale factor and surface area, create a poster that shows your answer and how to calculate it.	35		
	Investigate other space figures, such as icosahedrons and dodecahedrons. Develop a theory about how to calculate the total surface area of these figures. Create a poster that shows your findings with calculations to prove your thoughts.	40		
	You have been given the task of developing a surface area exhibit for the Children's Math Museum. This display should show various examples of surface area and how to calculate it. Be sure to have a few questions for visitors to answer as they examine the exhibit.	40		
	Use household objects to create an imaginary animal made out of geometric shapes that includes at least one of each of the following: cylinder, prism, cone, and sphere. Calculate its surface area and show your work.	40		
	Free choice: must be outlined on a proposal form and approved before beginning work.	10–40 points		
	Total number of points you are planning to earn from Side 1.	**Total points earned from Side 1:**		
	Total number of points you are planning to earn from Side 2.	**Total points earned from Side 2:**		
			Grand Total (/100)	

I am planning to complete _____ activities that could earn up to a total of _____ points.

Teacher's initials _____ Student's signature _____

Name:_____ Date:_____

Surface Area: Side 1

Guidelines:
1. You may complete as many of the activities listed as you can within the time period.
2. You may choose any combination of activities.
3. Your goal is 100 points. You may earn up to _____ points extra credit.
4. You may be as creative as you like within the guidelines listed below.
5. You must show your plan to your teacher by _____.
6. Activities may be turned in at any time during the working time period. They will be graded and recorded on this sheet as you continue to work, so keep it safe!

Plan to Do	Activity to Complete (Side 1: 15–20 points)	Point Value	Date Completed	Points Earned
	Create a mind map for the different solids and how we measure lateral surface area, total surface area, and volume for each. Be sure to include examples!	15		
	Create a set of concentration cards for matching the formulas for different space figures with drawings of the figures.	15		
	Make an acrostic for the term "surface area" in which you share what it is and why it is important to know.	15		
	Create a PowerPoint presentation that shows how to calculate the total and lateral surface areas of various space figures.	20		
	Create an instruction card for calculating lateral or total surface area of a solid for someone who is not sure what solid he or she is looking at or what any of the variables stand for. Be as specific as you can!	20		
	Create Three Facts and a Fib for the surface area of space figures.	20		
	Design a worksheet that focuses on situations where lateral or total surface area is calculated.	20		
	Using graph paper, create your own set of nets for various geometric shapes and show how you use them to calculate total surface area.	20		
	Total number of points you are planning to earn from Side 1.	**Total points earned from Side 1:**		

Name:_____ Date:_____ ●

Surface Area: Side 2

Plan to Do	Activity to Complete (Side 2: 30 points and up)	Point Value	Date Completed	Points Earned
	Make a math video that shows viewers examples of different solids that they might find in their homes, including lateral surface areas and total surface areas.	30		
	Develop a class lesson that teaches your classmates about the relationship between the surface area and the volume of an object.	30		
	Write and illustrate a children's book about a prism and its quest to have its total surface area calculated.	30		
	Your PE teacher has proposed a challenge: Figure out how many dimples are on a basketball. Using your knowledge of scale factor and surface area, create a poster that shows your answer and how to calculate it.	30		
	You have been given the task of developing a surface area exhibit for the Children's Math Museum. This display should show various examples of surface area, including how to calculate it. Be sure to have a few questions for visitors to answer as they examine it.	35		
	Investigate other space figures, such as icosahedrons and dodecahedrons. Develop a theory about how to calculate the total surface area of these figures. Create a poster that shows your findings with calculations to prove your thoughts.	35		
	Use household objects to create an imaginary animal made out of geometric shapes that includes at least one of each of the following: cylinder, prism, cone, and sphere. Calculate its surface area and show your work.	35		
	Free choice: must be outlined on a proposal form and approved before beginning work.	10–40 points		
	Total number of points you are planning to earn from Side 1.	**Total points earned from Side 1:**		
	Total number of points you are planning to earn from Side 2.	**Total points earned from Side 2:**		
		Grand Total (/100)		

I am planning to complete _____ activities that could earn up to a total of _____ points.

Teacher's initials _____ Student's signature _____

Pythagorean Theorem

Meal Menu ▲ and Tic-Tac-Toe Menu ●

Objectives Covered Through These Menus and These Activities

- Students will solve problems using the Pythagorean theorem.
- Students will provide real-world examples of the Pythagorean theorem.
- Students will understand the different ways the Pythagorean theorem can be represented.

Materials Needed by Students for Completion

- Poster board or large white paper
- Microsoft PowerPoint or other slideshow software
- Blank index cards (for trading cards) ▲
- Materials for models
- Internet access (for WebQuests)
- Materials for quiz boards (e.g., batteries, holiday lights, aluminum foil, tape) ▲

Special Notes on the Use of These Menus

This topic has two different menu formats: Meal menu and Tic-Tac-Toe menu. The Meal menu is specifically selected for its meal-oriented, Bloom's-based options, as it is easily broken into manageable bits. The menu can be cut into strips, each strip featuring its own meal, to be given to students. This way, once students have chosen and submitted the breakfast product for grading, they can move on to the lunch strip, and lastly, they can complete the dinner and dessert strips. Because this type of menu is designed to become more advanced as students move through the meals, teachers may choose to provide their students who have special needs with just the meals and save the dessert for enrichment.

These menus allow students to create a WebQuest. There are multiple versions and templates for WebQuests available on the Internet. Teachers should decide whether to specify a certain format or allow students to create one of their own choosing.

The triangle menu offers students the opportunity to create a quiz board. Quiz boards can range from simple to very complex, depending on the knowledge and ability of the student. Quiz boards work best when the teacher creates a "tester" that can be used to check any boards that are submitted. Basic instructions on how to create quiz boards and testers can be found at http://www.cesiscience.org/attachments/article/100/QuizBoardDirections.pdf.

Time Frame

- 2–3 weeks—Students are given the menus as the unit is started. As the teacher presents lessons throughout the week, he or she should refer back to the menu options associated with that content. The teacher will go over all of the options for that content and have students place check marks in the boxes that represent the activities they are most interested in completing. If students are using the Tic-Tac-Toe menu form, activities chosen and completed should make a column or row. If students are using the Meal menu form, students will complete one product from each meal, with dessert being an optional enrichment product. When students complete these patterns, they will have completed one activity from each content area, learning style, or level of Bloom's Revised taxonomy.
- 1 week—At the start of the unit, the teacher chooses the three activities he or she feels are most valuable for students. Stations can be set up in the classroom. These three activities are available for student choice throughout the week as regular instruction takes place.
- 1–2 days—The teacher chooses an activity from the menu to use with the entire class.

Suggested Forms

- All-purpose rubric
- Free-choice proposal form

Pythagorean Theorem

Directions: Choose one activity each for breakfast, lunch, and dinner. Dessert is an activity you can choose to do after you have finished your other meals. All products must be completed by: _____.

Breakfast

☐ There are different ways to represent the Pythagorean theorem. Create a poster to show them.

☐ Create a model that represents the Pythagorean theorem. Include one problem that your model can assist in solving.

☐ Design a set of trading cards for all of the important players in the Pythagorean theorem. Include information about the role that each plays.

Lunch

☐ Create four different word problems based on real-world applications of the Pythagorean theorem. Write your problems in a flipbook, placing your answers and how to solve the problems on another piece of paper.

☐ Create a quiz board of real-world problems that can be solved using the Pythagorean theorem. Be sure to show all of the calculations in the answer key.

☐ Consider all of the different real-world applications of the Pythagorean theorem. Create a PowerPoint presentation that showcases these applications with sample calculations for each.

Dinner

☐ Create a children's book that could be used to teach younger children about Pythagoras, his ideas, and how his theorem is used in the real world.

☐ Come to class as Pythagoras and share your ideas, your theorem, and how you use your theorem.

☐ Free choice—Submit a proposal about the Pythagorean theorem to your teacher for approval.

Dessert

☐ Use your creativity to write and perform a play about a situation that can be solved with calculation using the Pythagorean theorem. Try to avoid a classroom setting—be creative!

☐ Investigate a few different websites that discuss the history of the Pythagorean theorem and its practical uses. Create a WebQuest that introduces users to both of these.

Name:_____ Date:_____ ●

Pythagorean Theorem

Directions: Check the boxes you plan to complete. They should form a tic-tac-toe across or down. All products are due by: _____.

☐ *Make a Poster* There are different ways to represent the Pythagorean theorem. Create a poster to show them.	☐ *Design a PowerPoint Presentation* Consider all of the different real-world applications of the Pythagorean theorem. Create a PowerPoint presentation that showcases these applications with sample calculations for each.	☐ *You Be Pythagoras* Come to class as Pythagoras and share your ideas, your theorem, and how you use your theorem. Be sure to stay true to your time period in your examples.
☐ *Produce a Play* Use your creativity to write and perform a play about a situation that can be solved with calculations using the Pythagorean theorem. Try to avoid a classroom setting—be creative!	☐ **Free Choice: Pythagorean Theorem** (Fill out your proposal form before beginning the free choice!)	☐ *Design a Flipbook* Create five different word problems based on real-world applications of the Pythagorean theorem. Write your problems in a flipbook, placing your answers and how to solve the problems on another piece of paper.
☐ *Make a WebQuest* Investigate a few different websites that discuss the history of the Pythagorean theorem and its practical uses. Create a WebQuest that introduces users to both of these.	☐ *Write a Children's Book* Create a children's book that could be used to teach younger children about Pythagoras, his ideas, and how his theorem is used in the real world.	☐ *Make a Model* Create a model that represents the Pythagorean theorem. Include at least two problems that your model can assist in solving.

CHAPTER 7

Graphing and Measurement

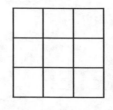

Graphing

Meal Menu ▲ and Tic-Tac-Toe Menu ●

Objectives Covered Through These Menus and These Activities

- Students will evaluate which graphs are best for showing certain types of data.
- Students will choose appropriate graphs to show their own data.
- Students will be able to create circle graphs, bar graphs, and histograms.

Materials Needed by Students for Completion

- Materials for board games (e.g., folders, colored cards)
- Microsoft PowerPoint or other slideshow software
- Scrapbooking materials (including newspapers and magazines)
- Large lined index cards (for recipe cards)
- Coat hangers (for mobiles)
- Blank index cards (for mobiles)
- String (for mobiles)

Special Notes on the Use of These Menus

This topic has two different menu formats: Meal menu and Tic-Tac-Toe menu. The Meal menu is specifically selected for its meal-oriented, Bloom's-based options, as it is easily broken into manageable bits. The menu can be cut into strips, each strip featuring its own meal, to be given to students. This way, once students have chosen and submitted the breakfast product for grading, they can move on to the lunch strip, and lastly, they can complete the dinner and dessert strips. Because this type of menu is designed to become more advanced as students move through the meals, teachers may choose to provide their students who have special needs with just the meals and save the dessert for enrichment.

Time Frame

- 2–3 weeks—Students are given the menus as the unit is started. As the teacher presents lessons throughout the week, he or she should refer back to the menu options associated with that content. The teacher will go over all of the options for that content and have students place check marks in the boxes that represent the activities they are most interested in completing. If students are using the Tic-Tac-Toe menu form, activities chosen and completed should make a column or row. If students are using the Meal menu form, students will complete one product from each meal, with dessert being an optional enrichment product. When students complete these patterns, they will have completed one activity from each content area, learning style, or level of Bloom's Revised taxonomy.

- 1 week—At the start of the unit, the teacher chooses the three activities he or she feels are most valuable for students. Stations can be set up in the classroom. These three activities are available for student choice throughout the week as regular instruction takes place.
- 1–2 days—The teacher chooses an activity from the menu to use with the entire class.

Suggested Forms

- All-purpose rubric
- Student-taught lesson rubric
- Free-choice proposal form

Graphing

Directions: Choose one activity each for breakfast, lunch, and dinner. Dessert is an activity you can choose to do after you have finished your other meals. All products must be completed by: _____.

Breakfast

❐ Build a mobile for graphing with at least four different types of graphs, examples of each type, and the best use for each type.

❐ Make a PowerPoint presentation that shows how to choose a graph based on the information you would like to present.

❐ Create a graphing mind map that shares the different types of graphs, what each type shows, and real-world examples of what might be recorded on each.

Lunch

❐ Create a survey that will provide data that could be shown on a circle graph. Have at least five people complete your survey and create your graph.

❐ Create a recipe card for making a histogram. Design a survey and use your card to create your own histogram out of your survey data.

❐ Design a survey that will provide information you could use to create a bar graph. Give your survey to at least five people and create a three-dimensional bar graph to show your data.

Dinner

❐ Look through the newspaper and magazines to find examples of different types of graphs. Create a scrapbook of these graphs. On each page, summarize the graphs and share at least one question that can be answered using each graph.

❐ Locate a bar graph and a line graph that show real-world data. Create two Three Facts and a Fibs, one for each graph.

❐ Free choice—Submit a proposal form about analyzing graphs to your teacher for approval.

Dessert

❐ Create a board game in which players analyze data presented on different types of graphs.

❐ Design a lesson for your classmates to help them figure out when to use each type of graph: circle, bar, line, and histogram.

Name:_____ Date:_____ ●

Graphing

Directions: Check the boxes you plan to complete. They should form a tic-tac-toe across or down. All products are due by: _____.

☐ *Make Your Own Graph* Create a survey that will provide data that could be shown on a circle graph. Have at least eight people complete your survey, and use the data to create your graph.	☐ *Which Graph Is Best?* Make a PowerPoint presentation that shows how to choose a graph based on the information you would like to present.	☐ *Analyzing Graphs* Create a board game in which players analyze data presented on different types of graphs.
☐ *Analyzing Graphs* Look through the newspaper and magazines to find examples of different types of graphs. Create a scrapbook of these graphs. On each page, summarize the graphs and share at least two questions that can be answered using each graph.	☐ **Free Choice: Make Your Own Graph** (Fill out your proposal form before beginning the free choice!)	☐ *Which Graph Is Best?* Design a lesson for your classmates to help them figure out when to use each type of graph: circle, bar, line, and histogram.
☐ *Which Graph Is Best?* Build a mobile for graphing with at least four different types of graphs, examples of each type, and the best use for that type.	☐ *Analyzing Graphs* Locate a bar graph and a line graph that show real-world data. Create two Three Facts and a Fibs, one for each graph.	☐ *Make Your Own Graph* Create a recipe card for making a histogram. Design a survey and use your card to create your own histogram out of your data.

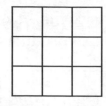

Coordinate Planes

Meal Menu ▲ and Tic-Tac-Toe Menu ●

Objectives Covered Through These Menus and These Activities

- Students will generate mathematically similar shapes by enlarging and reducing through dilation.
- Students will recognize translations and reflections in art and architecture.
- Students will locate and name points on a coordinate plane.

Materials Needed by Students for Completion

- Poster board or large white paper
- Information on M. C. Escher
- Graph paper (for drawings)
- Materials for bulletin board displays
- Large lined index cards (for instruction cards)
- Scrapbooking materials
- Materials for quiz boards (e.g., batteries, holiday lights, aluminum foil, tape)

Special Notes on the Use of These Menus

This topic has two different menu formats: Meal menu and Tic-Tac-Toe menu. The Meal menu is specifically selected for its meal-oriented, Bloom's-based options, as it is easily broken into manageable bits. The menu can be cut into strips, each strip featuring its own meal, to be given to students. This way, once students have chosen and submitted the breakfast product for grading, they can move on to the lunch strip, and lastly, they can complete the dinner and dessert strips. Because this type of menu is designed to become more advanced as students move through the meals, teachers may choose to provide their students who have special needs with just the meals and save the dessert for enrichment.

These menus offer students the opportunity to create a quiz board. Quiz boards can range from simple to very complex, depending on the knowledge and ability of the student. Quiz boards work best when the teacher creates a "tester" that can be used to check any boards that are submitted. Basic instructions on how to create quiz boards and testers can be found at http://www.cesiscience.org/attachments/article/100/QuizBoardDirections.pdf.

These menus also allow students to create a bulletin board display. Some classrooms may only have one bulletin board, so the teacher can divide the board into sections, or additional classroom wall or hall space can be sectioned off for the creation of these displays. Students can plan their displays based on the amount of space they are assigned.

Time Frame

- 2–3 weeks—Students are given the menus as the unit is started. As the teacher presents lessons throughout the week, he or she should refer back to the menu options associated with that content. The teacher will go over all of the options for that content and have students place check marks in the boxes that represent the activities they are most interested in completing. If students are using the Tic-Tac-Toe menu form, activities chosen and completed should make a column or row. If students are using the Meal menu form, students will complete one product from each meal, with dessert being an optional enrichment product. When students complete these patterns, they will have completed one activity from each content area, learning style, or level of Bloom's Revised taxonomy.
- 1 week—At the start of the unit, the teacher chooses the three activities he or she feels are most valuable for students. Stations can be set up in the classroom. These three activities are available for student choice throughout the week as regular instruction takes place.
- 1–2 days—The teacher chooses an activity from the menu to use with the entire class.

Suggested Forms

- All-purpose rubric
- Student-taught lesson rubric ●
- Free-choice proposal form

Coordinate Planes

Directions: Choose one activity each for breakfast, lunch, and dinner. Dessert is an activity you can choose to do after you have finished your other meals. All products must be completed by: _____.

Breakfast

❑ Your classmates feel they know all about ordered pairs. Create a worksheet for your classmates that will challenge them to practice plotting and finding points on a coordinate plane.

❑ Design a quiz board that has players match coordinates with their points on a coordinate plane. Be creative in its design!

❑ Create a song or rap that shows how to locate and name points on a graph. Make a graph to use while you perform the song.

Lunch

❑ Do reflections always have a line of symmetry? Create a poster that answers this question by sharing various examples.

❑ Architects often use translations and reflections of geometric shapes when they design their buildings. Create a scrapbook of local photographs or pictures from magazines that show this technique. Label the translations and reflections.

❑ Create a children's book about lines of symmetry and reflections found in living things. Use pictures rather than clip art whenever possible.

Dinner

❑ Create an instruction card that explains how to complete reductions and enlargements. Include an example of each on the back of your card.

❑ Dilations can be used to enlarge or reduce shapes on a coordinate plane. They can also be used to enlarge or reduce drawings by placing a reference grid over a drawing. Investigate this process, and after choosing a drawing, enlarge or reduce it at least twice.

❑ Free choice—Submit a proposal about dilations to your teacher for approval.

Dessert

❑ Using a piece of graph paper, make a drawing or picture. Write instructions directing other students to create your drawing using only the coordinates in the correct order.

❑ The artist M. C. Escher created some of his artwork using translations and tessellations of a symmetrical object. Research his works, and after choosing a symmetrical object that represents your personality, create your own masterpiece. Include a brief statement about how you used translations.

© Prufrock Press Inc. • *Differentiating Instruction With Menus for the Inclusive Classroom: Math • Grades 6–8*

Name:_____ Date:_____

Coordinate Planes

Directions: Check the boxes you plan to complete. They should form a tic-tac-toe across or down. All products are due by: _____.

☐ *Ordered Pairs* Design a quiz board that has players match coordinates with their points on a coordinate plane. Be creative in its design!	☐ *Translations and Reflections* M. C. Escher created some of his artwork using translations and tessellations of a symmetrical object. Research his works, choose a symmetrical object that represents your personality, and create your own masterpiece. Explain how you used translations.	☐ *Dilations* Design a lesson for your classmates that shows them examples of dilations as well as how to dilate a shape on a coordinate graph.
☐ *Dilations* Dilations can be used to enlarge or reduce shapes on a coordinate plane. They also can be used to enlarge or reduce drawings by placing a reference grid over a drawing. Investigate this process, and after choosing a drawing, enlarge or reduce it at least twice.	☐ **Free Choice: Ordered Pairs** (Fill out your proposal form before beginning the free choice!)	☐ *Translations and Reflections* Do reflections always have a line of symmetry? Create a bulletin board display that answers this question by sharing various examples.
☐ *Translations and Reflections* Architects often use translations and reflections of geometric shapes when they design their buildings. Create a scrapbook of local photographs or pictures from magazines that show this technique. Label the translations and reflections.	☐ *Dilations* Create an instruction card that explains how to complete reductions and enlargements. Include an example of each on the back of your card.	☐ *Ordered Pairs* Using a piece of graph paper, make a drawing or picture. Write instructions directing other students to create your drawing using only the coordinates in the correct order.

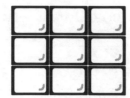

Transformations and Symmetry

Game Show Menus

Objectives Covered Through These Menus and These Activities

- Students will identify an object's line and rotational symmetry.
- Students will explain whether each transformation creates a congruent or a similar image.
- Students will recognize translations and reflections in art and architecture.
- Students will generate mathematically similar shapes by enlarging and reducing through dilation.

Materials Needed by Students for Completion

- Scrapbooking materials
- Graph paper (for drawings)
- Microsoft PowerPoint or other slideshow software ●
- Internet access (for WebQuests)
- Materials for bulletin board displays
- Large lined index cards (for instruction cards)
- Materials for board games (e.g, folders, colored cards) ▲

Special Notes on the Use of These Menus

These menus allow students to create a bulletin board display. Some classrooms may only have one bulletin board, so the teacher can divide the board into sections, or additional classroom wall or hall space can be sectioned off for the creation of these displays. Students can plan their displays based on the amount of space they are assigned.

These menus also allow students to create a WebQuest. There are multiple versions and templates for WebQuests available on the Internet. Teachers should decide whether to specify a certain format or allow students to create one of their own choosing.

Time Frame

- 2–3 weeks—Students are given the menus as the unit is started, and the guidelines and point expectations are discussed. As lessons are taught throughout the unit, students and the teacher can refer back to the options associated with the topic. The teacher will go over all of the options for the topic being covered and will have students place check marks in the boxes next to the activities they are most interested in completing. As teaching continues throughout the 2–3 weeks, activities are discussed, chosen, and submitted for grading.

- 1 week—At the beginning of the unit, the teacher chooses an activity from each area that he or she feels would be most valuable for students. Stations can be set up in the classroom. These activities are available for student choice throughout the week as regular instruction takes place.
- 1–2 days—The teacher chooses an activity from an objective to use with the entire class during lesson time.

Suggested Forms

- All-purpose rubric
- Point-based free-choice proposal form

Guidelines for Transformations and Symmetry Game Show Menu

- You must choose at least one activity from each topic area.
- You may not do more than two activities in any one topic area for credit. (You are, of course, welcome to do more than two for your own investigation.)
- Grading will be ongoing, so turn in products as you complete them.
- All free-choice proposals must be turned in and approved prior to working on that free-choice product.
- You must earn 100 points for a 100%. You may earn extra credit up to _____ points.
- You must show your teacher your plan for completion by: _____.

Transformations and Symmetry

Symmetry	Translations	Rotations	Dilations	Points for Each Level
☐ Create a scrapbook with at least eight different real-world examples of line and rotational symmetry. Label each with its type of symmetry, as well the line or point of rotation. (15 pts.)	☐ Create a folded quiz book about the different types of translations and how to draw them. (15 pts.)	☐ Create an instruction card that explains how to complete a rotation. Include an example of each step on the back of your card. (15 pts.)	☐ Create a worksheet that will give your classmates the opportunity to practice creating dilations. (15 pts.)	15 points
☐ Write a children's book about symmetry in the world around us. Be imaginative in the examples you choose and their explanations. (25 pts.)	☐ Create a board game in which players practice completing translations they are given. Your board should have a translation theme! (20 pts.)	☐ Design a bulletin board display that shows examples of rotations and how they are created. (25 pts.)	☐ Create Three Facts and a Fib about dilations and how to calculate their scale factor. (25 pts.)	20–25 points
☐ Most organisms in nature have either lateral (line) or radial (rotational) symmetry. After investigating some of these organisms, use graph paper to assist you in drawing a human with rotaticnal symmetry. (30 pts.)	☐ Tessellations are often used when designing buildings. Research this technique, and after choosing a symmetrical object that represents your personality, create a tessellation of your own that is at least 10 cm in length. Include a brief statement about how your artwork depends on translation. (30 pts.)	☐ There are many interactive websites that use games and simulations to teach rotations. Create a WebQuest that focuses on how to create and determine the symmetry of a rotation. (30 pts.)	☐ Dilations can be used to enlarge or reduce shapes using a coordinate plane. They can also be used to enlarge or reduce drawings by placing the coordinate plane over a drawing. Investigate this process, and after choosing a drawing, enlarge or reduce it at least twice. (30 pts.)	30 points
Free Choice (prior approval) (25–50 pts.)	**Free Choice** (prior approval) (25–50 pts.)	**Free Choice** (prior approval) (25–50 pts.)	**Free Choice** (prior approval) (25–50 pts.)	25–50 points
Total:	Total:	Total:	Total:	Total Grade:

Transformations and Symmetry

Symmetry	Translations	Rotations	Dilations	Points for Each Level
☐ Create a scrapbook with at least 10 different real-world examples of line and rotational symmetry. Label each with its type of symmetry, as well the line or point of rotation. (15 pts.)	☐ Create a folded quiz book about the different types of translations and how to draw them. (10 pts.)	☐ Create an instruction card that explains how to complete a rotation. Include an example of each step on the back of your card, as well as how rotations depend on symmetry. (15 pts.)	☐ Create a worksheet that will give your classmates the opportunity to practice creating dilations and identifying their scale factor. (15 pts.)	10–15 points
☐ Write a children's book about symmetry in the world around us. Be imaginative in the examples you choose and their explanations. (25 pts.)	☐ Choose at least two artists who use translations in their artwork. Create a PowerPoint presentation about their art and the importance of translations in their creations. (25 pts.)	☐ Create Three Facts and a Fib about rotations and how they are drawn and measured. (20 pts.)	☐ Design a bulletin board display that shows examples of dilations and how they are created. (20 pts.)	20–25 points
☐ Most organisms in nature have either lateral (line) or radial (rotational) symmetry. After investigating some of these organisms, use graph paper to assist you in drawing a human with rotational symmetry. (30 pts.)	☐ Tessellations are often used when designing buildings. Research this technique, and after choosing a symmetrical object that represents your personality, create a tessellation of your own that is at least 18 cm in length. Include a brief statement about how your artwork depends on translation. (30 pts.)	☐ There are many interactive websites that use games and simulations to teach rotations. Create a WebQuest that focuses on how to create and determine the symmetry of a rotation. (30 pts.)	☐ Dilations can be used to enlarge or reduce shapes using a coordinate plane. They can also be used to enlarge or reduce drawings by placing the coordinate plane over a drawing. Investigate this process, and after choosing a drawing, enlarge or reduce it at least twice. (30 pts.)	30 points
Free Choice (prior approval) (25–50 pts.)	Free Choice (prior approval) (25–50 pts.)	Free Choice (prior approval) (25–50 pts.)	Free Choice (prior approval) (25–50 pts.)	25–50 points
Total:	Total:	Total:	Total:	Total Grade:

Measurement

List Menu ▲ and Baseball Menu ●

Objectives Covered Through These Menus and These Activities

- Students will estimate length, capacity, weight, and temperature in standard and metric units.
- Students will solve problems using length, capacity, weight, and temperature in standard and metric units.
- Students will solve real-world problems using time and schedules.

Materials Needed by Students for Completion

- Poster board or large white paper
- Coat hangers (for mobiles)
- String (for mobiles)
- Blank index cards (for mobiles and concentration cards)
- Newspapers (for posters)
- Microsoft PowerPoint or other slideshow software
- Internet access (for research and scheduling)
- Graduated cylinders, measuring cups, triple beam balance, and spring scale
- Graph paper (for maps)
- Materials for museum exhibits (e.g., boxes, cards)
- Scrapbooking materials

Time Frame

- 2–3 weeks—Students are given the menus as the unit is started, and guidelines and point expectations are discussed. Usually, students are expected to complete 100 points. Because these menus cover one topic in depth, the teacher will go over all of the options for the topic being covered and have students place check marks in the boxes next to the activities they are most interested in completing. As instruction continues, activities are completed by students and submitted for grading.
- 1 week—At the beginning of the unit, the teacher chooses one or two higher level activities that can be integrated into whole-group instruction throughout the week.

- 1–2 days—The teacher chooses an activity from an objective to use with the entire class during lesson time.

Suggested Forms

- All-purpose rubric
- Point-based free-choice proposal form

Name:_____ Date:_____ ▲

Measurement: Side 1

Guidelines:

1. You may complete as many of the activities listed as you can within the time period.
2. You may choose any combination of activities.
3. Your goal is 100 points. You may earn up to _____ points extra credit.
4. You may be as creative as you like within the guidelines listed below.
5. You must show your plan to your teacher by _____.
6. Activities may be turned in at any time during the working time period. They will be graded and recorded on this sheet as you continue to work, so keep it safe!

Plan to Do	Activity to Complete (Side 1: 10–35 points)	Point Value	Date Completed	Points Earned
	Create a mobile with the different units for measuring length, weight, capacity, and temperature, as well as an example of an object that would best be measured with each unit.	10		
	Create a set of concentration cards that would allow players to match units with their measurements.	10		
	Create acrostics for capacity, length, and weight. Be sure to use units in your phrases!	15		
	Go through the newspaper to locate articles that give examples of length, weight, and capacity. Prepare a poster with at least 10 examples.	15		
	Certain household items have temperature restrictions for their use. Research why they have these restrictions and find eight examples of these items in your home. Prepare a poster that shows the items and how temperature affects them.	20		
	Create a "guess the measure" game. In this game, players will need to estimate and measure the lengths and weights of target items. Be creative in the design of the game.	30		
	Create a map of your room. (You may have to do some measuring!) Develop a scale for your map using appropriate units.	30		
	All household items that hold liquids need to be marked in both metric and standard units. Are these measurements really accurate? Develop a system to test the accuracy of both the standard and the metric measurements. Test two household items, and present your data in a table.	35		
	Design a measurement exhibit for the National Math Museum. Your exhibit should discuss how the units of measurement have changed over the years, with real-world examples of each measurement you mention.	35		
	Total number of points you are planning to earn from Side 1.	**Total points earned from Side 1:**		

Measurement: Side 2

Plan to Do	Activity to Complete (Side 2: 40 points and up)	Point Value	Date Completed	Points Earned
	A movie theater is holding a day-long marathon. Analyze the movie times of current films and create a schedule that allows you to see as many movies as possible within the day. You cannot leave one movie for another, and you cannot see the same movie twice!	40		
	The world has many time zones. Prepare a PowerPoint presentation that describes the reasons for time zones and why the zones are not always straight lines.	40		
	Create the perfect schedule for a 24-hour period. It should be designed for people your age. Note: You must go to school, and you must sleep!	40		
	Weight is often used in packaging, rather than counting items. How accurate is this method? Choose a product that is packaged based on weight in grams rather than on a count of the items and devise a way to confirm the accuracy of this method.	50		
	Design an experiment in which your classmates would practice estimating and measuring in milliliters and liters.	55		
	You are participating in a race around the world. Prepare a scrapbook that details your itinerary and a list of what you will bring with you—be specific, because weight matters! You must meet all of the criteria of the competition: • You must visit at least seven major airports and six continents. • You must get at least 8 hours of sleep every 24 hours, although you can sleep on a plane if the flight is longer than 8 hours. Otherwise, you must stay in a location 8 hours for sleep. Be sure you do not cut your flight too close, as taxis are not always reliable! • You must bring enough clothing to be able to change at least once every 24 hours, but you cannot exceed the 14-pound carry-on luggage limit used by some overseas airlines. You may need to weigh your clothing to be sure it does not exceed the limit.	100		
	Free choice: must be outlined on a proposal form and approved before beginning work.	10–55 points		
	Total number of points you are planning to earn from Side 1.	**Total points earned from Side 1:**		
	Total number of points you are planning to earn from Side 2.	**Total points earned from Side 2:**		
		Grand Total (/100)		

I am planning to complete _____ activities that could earn up to a total of _____ points.

Teacher's initials _____ Student's signature _____

Name:_____ Date:_____

Measurement

Directions: Look through the following choices and decide how you want to make your game add to 100 points. Singles are worth 10, Doubles are worth 30, Triples are worth 50, and a Home Run is worth 100. Choose any combination you want! Place a check mark next to each choice you are going to complete. Make sure that your points equal 100!

Singles—10 Points Each

❏ Create a mobile with the different units for measuring length, weight, capacity, and temperature, as well as an example of an object that would be best measured with each unit.

❏ Go through the newspaper to locate articles that give examples of length, weight, and capacity. Prepare a poster with at least 10 examples.

❏ Certain household items have temperature restrictions for their use. Research why they have these restrictions, and find eight examples of these items in your home. Prepare a poster that shows the items and how temperature affects them.

❏ Create a capacity and length collection. Collect two nontoxic household items that are measured in each of the following units: centimeters, inches, meters, cups, pints, quarts, and gallons. This will give you a total of 14 items to bring to class.

❏ Create acrostics for capacity, length, and weight. Be sure to use units in your phrases!

❏ Create a set of concentration cards that would allow players to match units with their measurements.

Doubles—30 Points Each

❏ Create a "guess the measure" game. In this game, players will need to estimate and measure the lengths and weights of target items. Be creative in the design of the game.

❏ There are many time zones around the world. Prepare a PowerPoint presentation that describes the reason for time zones and the reasons why the zones are not always straight lines.

❏ A movie theater is holding a day-long movie marathon for just $10. Analyze the movie times of current films, and create a schedule that allows you to see as many movies as possible within the day. You cannot leave one movie for another, and you cannot see the same movie twice!

❏ All household items that hold liquids need to be marked in both metric and standard units. Are these measurements really accurate? Develop a system to test the accuracy of both the standard and the metric measurements. Test four household items, and present your data in a table.

❏ Create a map of your room. (You may have to do some measuring!) Develop a scale for your map using appropriate units.

Doubles—30 Points Each (contiued)

❒ Design a measurement exhibit for the National Math Museum. Your exhibit should discuss how the units of measurement have changed over the years, with real-world examples of each measurement you mention.

Triples—50 Points Each

❒ Design an experiment in which your classmates would practice estimating and measuring in milliliters and liters.

❒ Develop a strategy that would help you accurately guess an object's weight in grams and ounces, as well as its length in inches and centimeters. Record your method and all of your trials, and be ready to show your skill to your classmates.

❒ Weight is often used in packaging, rather than counting items. How accurate is this method? Choose a product that is packaged based on weight in grams rather than on a count of the items, and devise a way to confirm the accuracy of this method.

❒ Create the perfect schedule for 4 days. It should be designed for people your age and all of the interests they have. Note: You must go to school, and you must sleep!

Home Run—100 Points

❒ You are participating in a challenge to race around the world. Prepare a scrapbook that details your itinerary, your suitcase choice, and a list of what you will bring with you on the trip—be specific, because weight matters! You must meet all of the criteria of the competition. The competition states:

  o You must visit at least seven major airports and six continents.
  o You must get at least 8 hours of sleep every 24 hours, although you can sleep on a plane if the flight is longer than 8 hours. Otherwise, you must stay in a location to get 8 hours of sleep. Be sure you do not cut your flight too close, as taxis are not always reliable!
  o You must bring enough clothing to be able to change at least once every 24 hours, but you cannot exceed the 14-pound carry-on luggage limit used by some overseas airlines. You may need to weigh your clothing to be sure it does not exceed the limit.
  o Your suitcase must not be larger than a total of 45 linear inches (length added to height added to width), so choose wisely.

I Chose:

_____ Singles (10 points each)

_____ Doubles (30 points each)

_____ Triples (50 points each)

_____ Home Run (100 points)

CHAPTER 8

Basic Algebra

Using Variables

20-50-80 Menus

Objectives Covered Through These Menus and These Activities
- Students will understand the purpose of a variable in a mathematical statement.
- Students will recognize the common variables used in formulas.

Materials Needed by Students for Completion
- Poster board or large white paper
- Blank index cards (for trading cards)
- Product cube template
- Materials for board games (e.g., folders, colored cards) ●
- Materials for trophies

Time Frame
- 1–2 weeks—Students are given the menus as the unit is started, and the teacher discusses all of the product options on the menus. As the different options are discussed, students will choose products that add to a total of 100 points. As the lessons progress, the teacher and students refer back to the menu options associated with the content being taught.
- 1–2 days—The teacher chooses an activity or product from the menu to use with the entire class.

Suggested Forms
- All-purpose rubric
- Point-based free-choice proposal form

Using Variables

Directions: Choose at least two activities from the menu below. The activities must total at least 100 points. Place a check mark next to each box to show which activities you will complete. All activities must be completed by: _____.

---

20 Points

❑ Make a set of trading cards for all of the variables you have used in formulas in the past year. For each variable, include the formulas impacted by that variable. Remember that a variable may be in more than one formula!

❑ Create a variable cube to help others become more familiar with the use of certain variables in equations. Users will roll the cube and name all of the formulas they can that contain that variable. Place a common variable on each side, and include an answer sheet with all of the formulas that include the variables on the cube.

---

50 Points

❑ Create Three Facts and a Fib about how variables can be used in an equation or formula.

❑ Make a Venn diagram to compare and contrast variables with regular letters. Include specific examples in your diagram.

❑ Create a song or rap on variables that focuses on what they are and how they are used.

❑ Free choice—Prepare a proposal form and submit your idea for approval.

---

80 Points

❑ Using variables in a mathematical statement can be confusing to students. Create a children's book that explains how and why they are used. Make the use of variables fun and easy to understand.

❑ The annual Variable Awards select a variable each year that has a significant impact on math. Decide which variable should get the award this year, create a trophy for this variable, and write a paragraph about why it was nominated.

Name: _____ Date: _____

Using Variables

Directions: Choose at least two activities from the menu below. The activities must total at least 100 points. Place a check mark next to each box to show which activities you will complete. All activities must be completed by: _____.

---

20 Points

❏ Make a set of trading cards for all of the variables you have used in formulas for the last 2 years. For each variable, include the formulas impacted by that variable. Remember that a variable may be in more than one formula!

❏ Create a variable cube to help others become more familiar with the use of certain variables in equations. Users will roll the cube and name all of the formulas they can that use that variable. Place a common variable on each side, and include an answer sheet with all of the formulas that include the variables on the cube.

---

50 Points

❏ Design a brochure that explains how to tell a variable from a regular letter. Include examples of how each is used and how to identify each one.

❏ Create Three Facts and a Fib about how variables can be used in an equation or formula.

❏ Create a board game on variables that focuses on what they are and how they are used.

❏ Free choice—Prepare a proposal form and submit your idea for approval.

---

80 Points

❏ Using variables in a mathematical statement can be confusing to students. Create a children's book that explains how and why they are used. Make the use of variables fun and easy to understand.

❏ The annual Variable Awards select a variable each year that has a significant impact on math. Decide which variable should get the award this year, create a trophy for this variable, and write its acceptance speech.

Using Variables Cube

Place common variables from formulas you use frequently on each side of the cube so users can roll the cube and practice naming the variable that appears. Use this pattern or create your own cube.

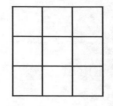

Algebraic Expressions

Meal Menu ▲ and Tic-Tac-Toe Menu ●

Objectives Covered Through These Menus and These Activities

- Students will match algebraic expressions with their verbal statement.
- Students will translate verbal phrases into algebraic expressions.
- Students will brainstorm the situations created through algebraic expressions.

Materials Needed by Students for Completion

- Blank index cards (for concentration cards)
- DVD or VHS recorder (for news reports and commercials)
- Materials for board games (e.g., folders, colored cards)
- Product cube template ▲
- Materials for quiz boards (e.g., batteries, holiday lights, aluminum foil, tape) ▲
- Scrapbooking materials (including newspapers and magazines)
- Product cube template ▲

Special Notes on the Use of These Menus

This topic has two different menu formats: Meal menu and Tic-Tac-Toe menu. The Meal menu is specifically selected for its meal-oriented, Bloom's-based options, as it is easily broken into manageable bits. The menu can be cut into strips, each strip featuring its own meal, to be given to students. This way, once students have chosen and submitted the breakfast product for grading, they can move on to the lunch strip, and lastly, they can complete the dinner and dessert strips. Because this type of menu is designed to become more advanced as students move through the meals, teachers may choose to provide their students who have special needs with just the meals and save the dessert for enrichment.

These menus give students the opportunity to create a news report or commercial. Although students enjoy producing their own videos, there are often difficulties obtaining the equipment and scheduling the use of the video recorder. The menus can be modified by allowing students to act out their videos (like a play), or if students have the technology, they may wish to produce a webcam or Flash version of their videos.

The triangle menu offers students the opportunity to create a quiz board. Quiz boards can range from simple to very complex, depending on the knowledge and ability of the student. Quiz boards work best when the teacher creates a "tester" that can be used to check any boards that are submitted. Basic instructions on how to create quiz boards and testers can be found at http://www.cesiscience.org/attachments/article/100/QuizBoardDirections.pdf.

Time Frame

- 2–3 weeks—Students are given the menus as the unit is started. As the teacher presents lessons throughout the week, he or she should refer back to the menu options associated with that content. The teacher will go over all of the options for that content and have students place check marks in the boxes that represent the activities they are most interested in completing. If students are using the Tic-Tac-Toe menu form, activities chosen and completed should make a column or row. If students are using the Meal menu form, students will complete one product from each meal, with dessert being an optional enrichment product. When students complete these patterns, they will have completed one activity from each content area, learning style, or level of Bloom's Revised taxonomy.
- 1 week—At the start of the unit, the teacher chooses the three activities he or she feels are most valuable for students. Stations can be set up in the classroom. These three activities are available for student choice throughout the week as regular instruction takes place.
- 1–2 days—The teacher chooses an activity from the menu to use with the entire class.

Suggested Forms

- All-purpose rubric
- Free-choice proposal form

Algebraic Expressions

Directions: Choose one activity each for breakfast, lunch, and dinner. Dessert is an activity you can choose to do after you have finished your other meals. All products must be completed by: _____.

Breakfast

❑ Brainstorm a list of situations and the algebraic expressions that might represent them. Create a set of concentration cards that allows users to match situations with expressions. Be sure to include addition, subtraction, multiplication, and division in your situations.

❑ Create a quiz board that quizzes your classmates on at least eight algebraic expressions and a real-world example of each.

❑ Create an algebraic expressions cube that has six different real-world situations on each side. When your classmates roll the cube, they should be able to write the algebraic expression for that side of the cube. Include an answer key for your cube.

Lunch

❑ Look through newspapers and magazines and collect examples of situations that could be expressed algebraically. Create a scrapbook for your examples and the algebraic expressions that accompany them.

❑ Create a worksheet that allows students to write algebraic expressions to match the situations you have provided.

❑ Brainstorm at least eight different situations that can be expressed through algebraic expressions. Use these situations to create a folded quiz book.

Dinner

❑ The same algebraic expression can be written in different ways. Create Three Facts and a Fib to practice this concept.

❑ Create an algebraic expressions board game in which players answer questions about writing and creating algebraic expressions.

❑ Free choice—Submit a proposal about algebraic expressions to your teacher for approval.

Dessert

❑ Consider the following algebraic expression: $c = 50x + 10$. Create a play that shows the situation behind this expression. Be expressive and creative in your story development.

❑ Create a commercial about a special bargain available to customers of a new store that just opened. The bargain is represented by: $82 - 2x$.

Name:_____ Date:_____

Algebraic Expressions

Directions: Check the boxes you plan to complete. They should form a tic-tac-toe across or down. All products are due by: _____.

☐ *Create Concentration Cards* Brainstorm a list of situations and the algebraic expressions that might represent them. Create a set of concentration cards that allows users to match them. Be sure to include addition, subtraction, multiplication, and division in your situations.	☐ *Contemplate a Commercial* Create a commercial about a special bargain available to customers of a new store that just opened. The bargain is represented by: $164 - 3x$.	☐ *Select a Scrapbook* Look through newspapers and magazines and collect examples of situations that could be expressed algebraically. Create a scrapbook for your examples and the algebraic expressions that accompany them.
☐ *Think Through Three Facts and a Fib* The same algebraic expression can be written in different ways. Create Three Facts and a Fib to practice this concept.	☐ **Free Choice: Algebraic Expressions** (Fill out your proposal form before beginning the free choice!)	☐ *Perform a Play* Consider the following algebraic expression: $c = 10x + 60$. Create a play that shows the situation behind this expression. Be expressive and creative in your story development.
☐ *Notify the News* Create a local news report that explains what is happening in the following algebraic expression: $4x + \$50.00$.	☐ *Build a Board Game* Create an algebraic expressions board game in which players answer questions about writing and creating algebraic expressions.	☐ *Fold a Quiz Book* Brainstorm at least 10 different situations that can be expressed through algebraic expressions. Use these situations to create a folded quiz book.

Algebraic Expressions Cube

Create an algebraic expressions cube that has six different real-world situations, one on each side. Include an answer key for your cube. Use this pattern or create your own cube.

Resources

Assouline, S. G., & Lupkowski-Shoplik, A. (2011). *Developing math talent: A comprehensive guide to math education for gifted students in elementary and middle school* (2nd ed.). Waco, TX: Prufrock Press.

Bollow, N., Berg, R., & Tyler, M. (2001). *Alien math.* Waco, TX: Prufrock Press.

Charlip, R. (1993). *Fortunately.* New York, NY: Aladdin.

Conway, J. H., & Guy, R. K. (1996). *The book of numbers.* New York, NY: Copernicus.

Fadiman, C. (1962). *The mathematical magpie.* New York, NY: Simon and Schuster.

Field, A. (2006). *The great math experience: Engaging problems for middle school mathematics.* Victoria, BC: Trafford.

Kleiman, A., & Washington, D. (with Washington, M. F.). (1996). *It's alive! Math like you've never known it before . . . and like you may never know it again.* Waco, TX: Prufrock Press.

Kleiman, A., & Washington, D. (with Washington, M. F.). (1996). *It's alive! And kicking!: Math the way it ought to be—tough, fun, and a little weird.* Waco, TX: Prufrock Press.

Lee, M., & Miller, M. (1997). *Real-life math investigations.* New York, NY: Scholastic.

Lee, M., & Miller, M. (2001). *40 fabulous math mysteries kids can't resist (grades 4–8)*. New York, NY: Scholastic.

Miller, M., & Lee, M. (1998). *Problem solving and logic: Great skill-building activities, games, and reproducibles*. New York, NY: Scholastic.

Pappas, T. (1993). *Fractals, googols, and other mathematical tales*. San Carlos, CA: Wide World Publishing.

Pappas, T. (1997). *Mathematical scandals*. San Carlos, CA: Wide World Publishing.

Schwartz, D. M. (1998). *G is for googol: A math alphabet book*. Berkeley, CA: Tricycle Press.

Scieszka, J., & Smith, L. (1995). *Math curse*. New York, NY: Viking.

Tyler, M. W. (1995). *Real life math mysteries: A kid's answer to the question, "What will we ever use this for?"* Waco, TX: Prufrock Press.

Zaccaro, E. (2003). *Primary grade challenge math*. Bellevue, IA: Hickory Grove Press.

Zaccaro, E. (2003). *The 10 things all future mathematicians and scientists must know (but are rarely taught)*. Bellevue, IA: Hickory Grove Press.

Zaccaro, E. (2005). *Challenge math for the elementary and middle school student* (2nd ed.). Bellevue, IA: Hickory Grove Press.

Zaccaro, E. (2006). *Becoming a problem solving genius*. Bellevue, IA: Hickory Grove Press.

References

Anderson, L., & Krathwohl, D. (Eds.). (2001). *A taxonomy for learning, teaching, and assessing: A revision of Bloom's taxonomy for educational objectives* (Complete ed.). New York, NY: Longman.

Mercer, C. D., Lane, H. B., Jordan, L., Allsopp, D. H., & Eisele, M. R. (1996). Empowering teachers and students with instructional choices in inclusive settings. *Remedial & Special Education, 17,* 226–236.

About the Author

After teaching science for more than 15 years, both overseas and in the U.S., **Laurie E. Westphal** now works as an independent gifted education and science consultant nationwide. She enjoys developing and presenting staff development on differentiation for various districts and conferences, working with teachers to assist them in planning and developing lessons to meet the needs of all students. Laurie currently resides in Houston, TX, and has made it her goal to convert as many teachers as she can to the differentiated lifestyle in the classroom and share her vision for real-world, product-based lessons that help all students become critical thinkers and effective problem solvers.

If you are interested in having Laurie speak at your next staff development day or conference, please visit her website, http://www.giftedconsultant.com, for additional information.

Additional Titles by the Author

Laurie E. Westphal has written many books on using differentiation strategies in the classroom, providing teachers of grades K–8 with creative, engaging, ready-to-use resources. Among them are:

Differentiating Instruction With Menus, Grades K–2
(Math, Language Arts, Science, and Social Studies volumes available)

Differentiating Instruction With Menus, Grades 3–5
(Math, Language Arts, Science, and Social Studies volumes available)

Differentiating Instruction With Menus, Grades 6–8
(Math, Language Arts, Science, and Social Studies volumes available)

Differentiating Instruction With Menus for the Inclusive Classroom, Grades K–2
(Math, Language Arts, Science, and Social Studies volumes available Spring 2013)

Differentiating Instruction With Menus for the Inclusive Classroom, Grades 3–5
(Math, Language Arts, Science, and Social Studies volumes available)

Differentiating Instruction With Menus for the Inclusive Classroom, Grades 6–8
(Math, Language Arts, Science, and Social Studies volumes available)

**For a current listing of Laurie's books, please visit
Prufrock Press at http://www.prufrock.com.**